English Grammar in Use
Supplementary Exercises

with answers

To accompany *English Grammar in Use Fourth Edition*

Louise Hashemi
with Raymond Murphy

CAMBRIDGE
UNIVERSITY PRESS

University Printing House, Cambridge CB2 8BS, United Kingdom

One Liberty Plaza, 20th Floor, New York, NY 10006, USA

477 Williamstown Road, Port Melbourne, VIC 3207, Australia

4843/24, 2nd Floor, Ansari Road, Daryaganj, Delhi – 110002, India

79 Anson Road, #06–04/06, Singapore 079906

Cambridge University Press is part of the University of Cambridge.

It furthers the University's mission by disseminating knowledge in the pursuit of education, learning and research at the highest international levels of excellence.

www.cambridge.org
Information on this title: www.cambridge.org/englishgrammarinuse

© Cambridge University Press 2012

This publication is in copyright. Subject to statutory exception and to the provisions of relevant collective licensing agreements, no reproduction of any part may take place without the written permission of Cambridge University Press.

First published 2012
20 19 18 17 16 15 14 13 12 11 10 9

Printed in Malaysia by Vivar Printing

A catalogue record for this publication is available from the British Library

ISBN 978-1-107-61641-7 English Grammar in Use Supplementary Exercises with answers
ISBN 978-1-107-63043-7 English Grammar in Use Supplementary Exercises without answers
ISBN 978-0-521-18906-4 Edition with answers
ISBN 978-0-521-18908-8 Edition without answers
ISBN 978-0-521-18939-2 Edition with answers and CD-ROM
ISBN 978-0-511-96173-1 Online access code pack
ISBN 978-1-107-64138-9 Online access code pack and book with answers

Cambridge University Press has no responsibility for the persistence or accuracy of URLs for external or third-party internet websites referred to in this publication, and does not guarantee that any content on such websites is, or will remain, accurate or appropriate. Information regarding prices, travel timetables and other factual information given in this work is correct at the time of first printing but Cambridge University Press does not guarantee the accuracy of such information thereafter.

Contents

To the student v
To the teacher v
Thanks vi

Exercise numbers		Page
1–10	Present continuous and present simple (**I am doing** and **I do**)	2
11–17	Past simple and past continuous (**I did** and **I was doing**)	7
18–22	Present and past (**I do / I am doing** and **I did / I was doing**)	11
23–28	Present perfect simple and continuous (**I have done** and **I have been doing**)	14
29–30	Present perfect simple and continuous; past simple (**I have done** and **I have been doing**; **I did**)	18
31–34	Present perfect and present (**I have done / I have been doing** and **I do / I am doing**)	19
35–36	Present perfect, present and past (**I have done / I have been doing**, **I do / I am doing** and **I did**)	22
37–42	Present perfect and past simple (**I have done / I have been doing** and **I did**)	23
43–46	Past simple, past continuous and past perfect (**I did**, **I was doing** and **I had done / I had been doing**)	27
47–51	Past simple, past continuous and **used to** (**I did**, **I was doing** and **I used to do**)	30
52–53	Present, present perfect and past	33
54–58	The future: present tenses and **will/shall** (**I do / I am doing** and **I will/shall do**)	34
59–63	The future: present continuous, **will/shall**, **going to** (**I am doing**, **I will/shall do** and **I am going to do**)	37
64	The future: all forms	40
65–66	**Can, could** and **be able to**	41
67–68	**May** and **might**	42
69–72	**Can, could, may, might, must** and **can't**	43
73–78	**Must(n't), need(n't), should(n't)** and **don't have to**	45
79–82	**(Don't) have to, should(n't), had better (not)** and **ought (not) to**	48

83–85	Should	50
86–87	Modals: review	52
88–93	**If I do** and **If I did**	53
94–97	**If I did** and **If I had done**	56
98–99	Conditionals: review	59
100–102	I wish	60
103–113	The passive	63
114–115	Have something done	71
116–120	Questions	72
121–131	Reported speech and questions	75
132–137	–ing and infinitive	82
138–140	Prepositions and expressions + –ing	86
141	**I'm used to doing** and **I used to do**	87
142	**To ...** and preposition + –ing (**Afraid to do** and **afraid of doing**)	88
143	Verb forms: review	89
144–148	Countable and uncountable	92
149–151	**A/an, some** and **the**	94
152–154	**The**	96
155–159	Quantifiers and pronouns	97
160–163	Relative clauses	100
164–165	Adjectives and adverbs	103
166–168	Comparatives and superlatives	104
169–172	Word order	106
173–175	Prepositions of time	108
176–177	Prepositions of place	110
178–179	Prepositions (general)	111
180–182	Adjective / verb + preposition	112
183–200	Phrasal verbs	113

Solution to Exercise 143   120

Key   121

To the student

English Grammar in Use Supplementary Exercises is for intermediate and advanced students who want extra practice in grammar, without help from a teacher.

There are 200 exercises in this new edition. Each exercise relates to a unit or units in *English Grammar in Use Fourth Edition*, with the unit number(s) at the top of the page. All the answers are given in the Key (pages 121–137). Some exercises ask you to use your own ideas. For these, you can check the *Example answers* in the Key. You can use this book if you don't have *English Grammar in Use*, but for an explanation of the grammar points, you need to check in *English Grammar in Use*.

The grammar points covered in this book are *not* in order of difficulty, so you can go straight to the parts where you need the most practice. Where there are several exercises on one grammar point, however, the easier ones come first. It's a good idea to do each exercise, check your answers and then go on to the next one.

Many of the exercises are in the form of emails, notes, conversations or short articles. You can use these as models for writing or speaking practice.

To the teacher

English Grammar in Use Supplementary Exercises offers extra practice of most of the grammar points covered in *English Grammar in Use Fourth Edition*. Much of the language is contextualised within dialogues, emails, notes, articles, etc., encouraging students to consider meaning as well as form. The book can be used as self-study material or as a basis for further practice in class or as homework.

The book is designed for students who have already worked through the exercises in *English Grammar in Use* (or elsewhere) which are relevant to their needs, but who need more, or more challenging, practice. It is particularly useful for revision work.

The exercises are organised in the same order as the units of *English Grammar in Use*, and the numbers of the relevant *English Grammar in Use* units are shown at the top of each page. Within each group of exercises there is a progression from easier to more challenging, including exercises where students are encouraged to use their own ideas. The contextualised exercises can be used as models or springboards for speaking and writing practice of a freer nature.

Thanks

The authors would like to thank Annabel Marriott of Cambridge University Press for advice and support during the writing of this new edition, and Rhona Snelling for great editing and many helpful suggestions. Also, everyone at Kamae for their creative design work.

For trying out exercises and providing valuable feedback on the first and second editions, thanks go to: students and staff at The British Council Young Learners' Centre, Barcelona, Spain, Anglo World, Cambridge, The Studio School, Cambridge, The International Language Academy, Cambridge, Lelio Pallini, Jon Butt, Cemille Iskenderoglu, Isidro Almándarez, Catherine Carpenter, Marco Palladino, Margarida C.T. Busatto, Katie Head, Aleya Mokhtar, Graham Palmer, Rob Waring.

Illustrations by: Kathy Baxendale, Humberto Blanco, Sandy Nichols, Roger Penwill, and Gary Wing.

The authors and publishers acknowledge the following sources of copyright material and are grateful for the permissions granted. While every effort has been made, it has not always been possible to identify the sources of all the material used, or to trace all copyright holders. If any omissions are brought to our notice, we will be happy to include the appropriate acknowledgements on reprinting.

The publishers are grateful to the following for permission to reproduce photographic material:

p.2TL: Rex Features/Philippe Hays; p.2CL: Thinkstock/Hemera; p.2BL: Shutterstock/ ArtmannWitte; p.2TR: Thinkstock/istockphoto; p.2CR: Thinkstock/istockphoto; p.2BR: Alamy/ Juice Images; p.3: David Hockney "Mr & Mrs Clark & Percy" 1970-71, acrylic on canvas, 84" x 120" ©David Hockney Collection: Tate Gallery p.6B: Shutterstock/ Photodynamic; p.6T: Shutterstock/Eky Studio; p.10: Thinkstock/Digital Vision; p.14: Shutterstock/gary718; p.15: Thinkstock/Comstock; p.19: Corbis/Jim Craigmyle; p.20: Shutterstock/S.Borisov; p.21: Alamy/ Colin Underhill; p.24T: Rex Features/ Rex Interstock; p.25B: Alamy/Pixellover RM 6; p.30: Alamy/Trinity Mirror/Mirrorpix; p.34: Alamy/Andrew Woodley; p.45: Corbis/Ocean; p.51: Alamy/Tetra Images; p.52: Shutterstock/Andresr; p.57: Corbis; p.63(1): Thinkstock/istockphoto; p.63(2): The Kobal Collection/Walt Disney Pictures; p.63(3): Thinkstock/istockphoto; p.63(4): Shutterstock/huntz; p.63(5): ©Succession Picasso/Dacs, London 2011, The Bridgeman Art Library/Museo Nacional Centro de Arte Reina Sofia, Madrid, Spain; p.63(6): Thinkstock/ istockphoto; p.63(7): Thinkstock/Stockbyte; p.63(8): Thinkstock/istockphoto; p.63(9): Shutterstock/ Dave Newman; p.63(10): Shutterstock/ itsmejust; p.65: Thinkstock/istockphoto; p.68: Colorport; p.70: Thinkstock/Creatas; p.73: Alamy/Simon Holdcroft; p.83: Shutterstock/ Ljupco Smokovski; p.87: Shutterstock/Christophe Testi; p.94: Alamy/incamerastock; p.95: Alamy/Greg Balfour Evans; p.96: Alamy/Radius Images; p.99: Alamy/Paul Broadbent; p.109: Alamy/moodboard; p.110: Thinkstock/istockphoto; p.116T: Shutterstock/aquatic creature; p.116B: Shutterstock/Monkey Business Images; p.117T: Shutterstock/Minerva Studio; p.117B: Alamy/Mark Richardson.

English Grammar in Use

Supplementary Exercises

with answers

Present continuous and present simple
(**I am doing** and **I do**)

Units 1–4, 19, 25

1 Complete the webpage with the present continuous form of the verbs from the box.

> hold   offer   organise   ~~perform~~   play   sing

What's on in Hampton this week?

The Arena
The world famous Company of Knights (1) *is performing* a breathtaking horseback show from Wednesday to Saturday at 7.30 pm.

City Hall
Elisa Gonzalez (2) .... songs from Brazil, Argentina and Mexico on Friday at 7 pm.

Hampton Sports Stadium
Hampton Juniors football team (3) .... against a team from Germany at 11 am on Sunday.

The Pavilion
Local jewellers (4) .... their Summer Sale this Sunday from 10 am to 2 pm.

Shoppers' Paradise (off Main Street)
All shoe shops (5) .... the chance to buy one pair get one pair free every day this week!

Hampton College of Further Education
The education department (6) .... an open day on Thursday – discover their range of full- and part-time courses.

2 Complete the sentences with the present continuous form of the verbs.

A JAN: Hi, Wendy! (1) *Are you waiting* .... (you / wait) for the London train?
WENDY: No, (2) .... (I / meet) my mother off the train from Bristol.

B MANDY: (3) .... (this music / disturb) you?
JAMES: No, not at all. (4) .... (I / enjoy) it.

C TOM: (5) .... (anyone / use) this room today?
ELLIE: (6) .... (We / have) a meeting here after lunch, but it's free now.

D NINA: Why (7) .... (those people / shout)?
FINN: (8) .... (They / demonstrate) against the government.

E BEN: (9) .... (you / apply) for university?
CRAIG: (10) .... (I / think) about it, but I haven't decided yet.

F SINDY: (11) .... (Jane / leave) work early today?
KATE: Yes, (12) .... (she / fly) to Brussels at five o'clock.

G JOSH: (13) .... (you / come) to the party on Thursday?
MAX: No, (14) .... (I / work) late, unfortunately.

English Grammar in Use Supplementary Exercises

Present continuous and present simple

Units 1–4, 19, 25

3 Complete the description with the present continuous form of suitable verbs. Use the negative where necessary.

Mr and Mrs Clark and Percy by David Hockney, 1970

This is a painting of two people and their cat. Mr Clark (1) ......*is sitting*...... on a chair. Mrs Clark (2) .... near him. They (3) .... at each other, but at the viewer. Mrs Clark (4) .... a long dress. Mr Clark's got trousers and a jumper, but he (5) .... shoes. Percy is on Mr Clark's lap and he (6) .... something in the garden. The sun (7) .... outside, but the room is a bit dark. We can see part of a picture which (8) .... on the wall behind Mrs Clark. There's a vase of lilies on the table, and a book (9) .... beside it.

4 Choose a picture or photograph you like and describe what is happening in it.

....
....
....
....
....
....
....

Present continuous and present simple

Units 1–4, 19, 25

5 Complete the text with the present simple form of the verbs.

What is an eclipse?

A solar eclipse (1) _happens_ (happen) when the moon (2) _____ (pass) in front of the sun. This only (3) _____ (take) place when there is a new moon. It (4) _____ (last) for up to 7.5 minutes.

During a solar eclipse, it is dark. The birds (5) _____ (not sing), and animals (6) _____ (keep) still and quiet. A solar eclipse (7) _____ (not happen) very often, and most people (8) _____ (enjoy) seeing one. However, it's important not to look straight at the sun. If you (9) _____ (not remember) this, you can damage your eyes.

A lunar eclipse (10) _____ (occur) when the earth's shadow (11) _____ (fall) on the moon. The moon (12) _____ (look) dim until it (13) _____ (come) out from the shadow.

6 Complete the questions with the present simple form of the verbs.

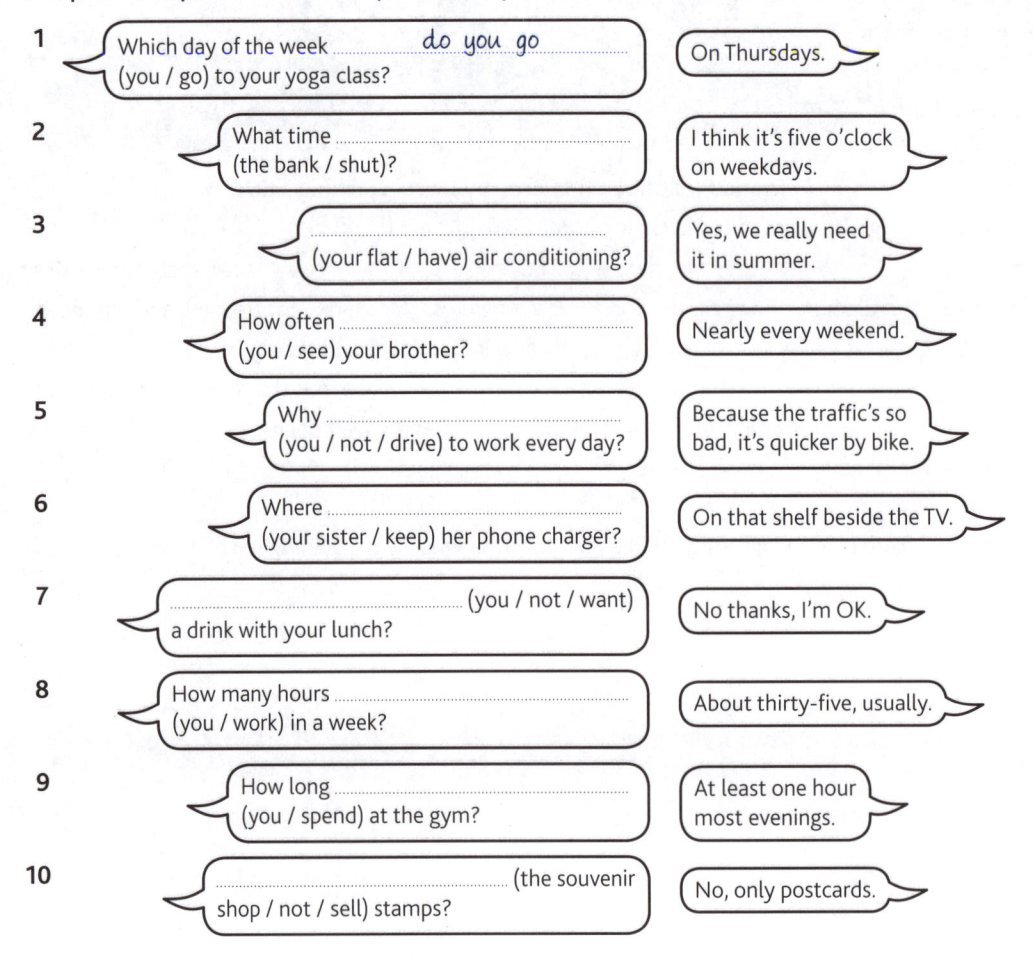

1 Which day of the week _do you go_ (you / go) to your yoga class? — On Thursdays.

2 What time _____ (the bank / shut)? — I think it's five o'clock on weekdays.

3 _____ (your flat / have) air conditioning? — Yes, we really need it in summer.

4 How often _____ (you / see) your brother? — Nearly every weekend.

5 Why _____ (you / not / drive) to work every day? — Because the traffic's so bad, it's quicker by bike.

6 Where _____ (your sister / keep) her phone charger? — On that shelf beside the TV.

7 _____ (you / not / want) a drink with your lunch? — No thanks, I'm OK.

8 How many hours _____ (you / work) in a week? — About thirty-five, usually.

9 How long _____ (you / spend) at the gym? — At least one hour most evenings.

10 _____ (the souvenir shop / not / sell) stamps? — No, only postcards.

Present continuous and present simple

Units 1–4, 19, 25

7 Choose the correct alternative.

From: Pedro Martinez pm3@rygl.com
To: Kai Muller
Date: September 5, 2012
Subject: Hi from Canada

Hi Kai

(1) <u>I'm having / I have</u> a great time here in Canada. My MSc course (2) <u>isn't starting / doesn't start</u> until next month, so (3) <u>I'm making / I make</u> use of the time to get to know the place. (4) <u>I'm staying / I stay</u> near Vancouver with Ryan, my Canadian cousin. He and and his brother Glen (5) <u>are owning / own</u> a software business. In the evenings (6) <u>we're driving / we drive</u> into the city and go clubbing or see a movie. (7) <u>I'm making / I make</u> a lot of new friends. (8) <u>I'm thinking / I think</u> my pronunciation is much better already, and (9) <u>I'm understanding / I understand</u> almost everything. On weekdays (10) <u>I'm helping / I help</u> Glen. At the moment (11) <u>he's working / he works</u> on their new website and (12) <u>he's needing / he needs</u> help with it. (13) <u>I'm learning / I learn</u> some useful stuff about how people (14) <u>are doing / do</u> business in this country. (15) <u>Do you come / Are you coming</u> to see me? (16) <u>I'm spending / I spend</u> the winter holiday skiing with Ryan and Glen. (17) <u>They're wanting / They want</u> to meet you and there's plenty of space. You must bring lots of warm clothes because (18) <u>it's getting / it gets</u> really cold here in the winter. Let me know as soon as (19) <u>you're deciding / you decide</u>. And tell me what (20) <u>you're doing / you do</u> these days.
See you in December, I hope.
Pedro

8 Choose words from the box and make sentences ending as shown. Use verbs in the present continuous or present simple and any other words you need.

I	My best friend	My boss	My boyfriend	My classmates	My family
My father	My sister	My wife	None of my friends	Our children
Our next-door neighbour	Our teacher	Several of my colleagues

1 *My boyfriend is studying for his final exams* .... this term.
2 *My sister doesn't go to the cinema* .... very often.
3 *My classmates aren't talking much* .... right now.
4 .... this year.
5 .... every week.
6 .... at the moment.
7 .... this year.
8 .... at weekends.
9 .... this term.
10 .... right now.

Present continuous and present simple

Units 1–4, 19, 25

9 Put the verbs into the correct form: present continuous or present simple.

Tony Hunt, a journalist, is interviewing Leila Markham, an environmental scientist.

TONY: So tell me, Leila, why is it important to save the rainforests?

LEILA: There are so many reasons. One reason is that lots of the plants which (1) ...grow... (grow) in the rainforest could be useful in medicine.
We (2) .... (not / know) all the plants, but there are tens of thousands of them. Chemists and doctors (3) .... (try) to discover their secrets before they are destroyed.

TONY: I see. What other reasons are there?

LEILA: Well, scientists (4) .... (believe) that the rainforests (5) .... (have) an influence on the world's weather systems and this (6) .... (help) to slow down global warming. But, unfortunately, these days the forests (7) .... (disappear) at a terrifying rate and we (8) .... (not / do) enough to save them.

TONY: What is the main danger of global warming, in your opinion?

LEILA: The polar regions (9) .... (consist) of millions of tons of ice. If they (10) .... (melt), the level of the sea will rise and cause terrible floods. Most scientists (11) .... (agree) that global temperatures (12) .... (already / rise). We must do everything we can to prevent global warming, and that includes preserving the rainforests!

TONY: Thank you, Leila, and good luck in your campaign.

LEILA: Thank you.

10 Tick (✓) the sentences which are correct. In some pairs, one sentence is correct. In other pairs, both sentences are correct.

1	What do you think of my hair? ✓	What are you thinking of my hair?
2	You look great today!	You're looking great today!
3	Do you enjoy your meal?	Are you enjoying your meal?
4	I think of selling my car.	I'm thinking of selling my car.
5	Where do you live?	Where are you living?
6	I don't believe his story.	I'm not believing his story.
7	The students seem tired today.	The students are seeming tired today.
8	He weighs 80 kilos.	He's weighing 80 kilos.
9	How often do you play tennis?	How often are you playing tennis?
10	My brother looks for a new job.	My brother is looking for a new job.

English Grammar in Use Supplementary Exercises

Past simple and past continuous
(I did and I was doing)

Units 5–6, 17

11 Last week John went to Scotland on a business trip. Read his diary for last week. Then complete the report he sent to his boss using the past simple.

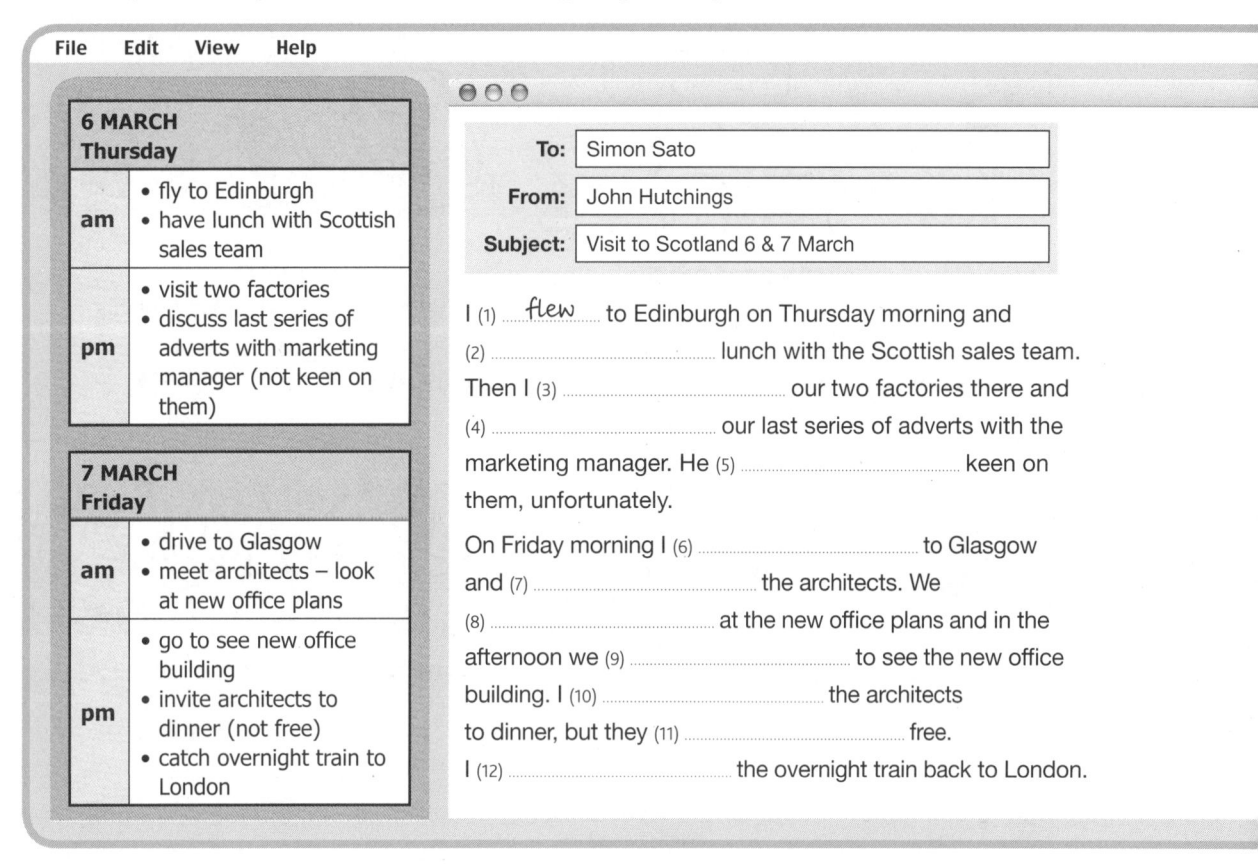

	6 MARCH Thursday	
am	• fly to Edinburgh • have lunch with Scottish sales team	
pm	• visit two factories • discuss last series of adverts with marketing manager (not keen on them)	

	7 MARCH Friday	
am	• drive to Glasgow • meet architects – look at new office plans	
pm	• go to see new office building • invite architects to dinner (not free) • catch overnight train to London	

To: Simon Sato
From: John Hutchings
Subject: Visit to Scotland 6 & 7 March

I (1) ...flew... to Edinburgh on Thursday morning and (2) .... lunch with the Scottish sales team. Then I (3) .... our two factories there and (4) .... our last series of adverts with the marketing manager. He (5) .... keen on them, unfortunately.

On Friday morning I (6) .... to Glasgow and (7) .... the architects. We (8) .... at the new office plans and in the afternoon we (9) .... to see the new office building. I (10) .... the architects to dinner, but they (11) .... free. I (12) .... the overnight train back to London.

12 Think about what you did one day last week. Complete the diary below. Then write a report using the past simple.

am	
lunch	
pm	
dinner	
evening	

Day:
Name:
On .... morning ....

Past simple and past continuous — Units 5–6, 17

13 Use the words given to make sentences. Do not change the order of the words. Use only the past simple or past continuous.

1. Katie / phone / the restaurant when the pizza / arrive
   Katie phoned the restaurant when the pizza arrived.

2. when Danny / arrive / we / pay / the bill
   When Danny arrived, we were paying the bill.

3. while he / walk / in the mountains, Harry / see / a bear

4. the students / play / a game when the professor / arrive

5. Felix / phone / the fire brigade when the cooker / catch fire

6. when the starter / fire her pistol / the race / begin

7. I / walk / home when it / start / to snow

8. Andy / have / lunch in a cafe when Juno / phone

English Grammar in Use Supplementary Exercises

Past simple and past continuous

Units 5–6, 17

14 Choose the correct alternative.

Lucky accidents

Is it true that Sir Isaac Newton understood gravity because an apple (1) <u>fell</u> / <s>was falling</s> on his head when he (2) <u>lay / was lying</u> under a tree in his garden? Probably not. However, many great and small discoveries are the result of lucky accidents …

One day in 1879 chemist Constantin Fahlberg (3) <u>didn't wash / wasn't washing</u> his hands before dinner. While he (4) <u>ate / was eating</u> he (5) <u>noticed / was noticing</u> that the bread (6) <u>tasted / was tasting</u> sweet. The sweetness was saccharin.

Alexander Fleming (7) <u>became / was becoming</u> interested in the control of bacteria while he (8) <u>worked / was working</u> as a doctor during the First World War. In 1928 he (9) <u>tidied / was tidying</u> his laboratory when he (10) <u>saw / was seeing</u> that one of the dirty dishes (11) <u>didn't have / wasn't having</u> any bacteria on it, but that something else (12) <u>grew / was growing</u> there. It was penicillin.

In 1930 dietician Ruth Wakefield (13) <u>prepared / was preparing</u> some cookies for guests when she (14) <u>realised / was realising</u> that she had no chocolate powder. She (15) <u>decided / was deciding</u> to use small pieces of ordinary chocolate instead. The chocolate pieces (16) <u>didn't melt / wasn't melting</u>, and the first chocolate chip cookies were a great success.

Dr Percy Spencer was a physicist in the 1940s who probably enjoyed chocolate chip cookies. He (17) <u>walked / was walking</u> past some equipment in the laboratory when he (18) <u>felt / was feeling</u> something strange in his pocket. It was his chocolate bar and it (19) <u>melted / was melting</u>. This accident (20) <u>led / was leading</u> to the invention of a new piece of cooking equipment – the microwave oven.

15 Put the verbs into the correct form: past simple or past continuous.

Hi Becky,

Guess what, my sister Naomi is married! She (1) ...<u>got</u>... (get) home from her round the world trip last week with a husband!! She (2) .... (meet) him when she (3) .... (travel) round New Zealand. One afternoon, while her friends (4) .... (shop), she (5) .... (go) to look round an art gallery. She (6) .... (look) at a small sculpture when a young man (7) .... (come) into the room and he (8) .... (start) to put it into his rucksack. She (9) .... (call) the security guard because she (10) .... (think) the man (11) .... (try) to steal it. She (12) .... (be) really embarrassed to discover that he (13) .... (not steal) it – it (14) .... (belong) to him! Anyway, he (15) .... (not mind) and he (16) .... (ask) her to go for a coffee. They (17) .... (get married) a month later in Bali. We (18) .... (not know) anything about it! Can you believe it? He's really nice and they are very happy together!

Love, Ada

Past simple and past continuous

Units 5–6, 17

16 Here is part of the website of a rock star called Colin Boyle. Put the verbs into the correct form: past simple or past continuous.

★ **COLIN BOYLE** HOME | NEWS | ABOUT | TOURS | EXTRAS

Colin Boyle was born in 1988 near Dublin, Ireland. In 2003 he became seriously ill. While he (1) _was recovering_ (recover), his uncle (2) _____ (give) him an old drumkit. He enjoyed playing and practised in a friend's garage every evening. One day in 2005, John Leaf, the manager of several successful musicians, (3) _____ (pass) the garage when he (4) _____ (hear) Colin practising. He (5) _____ (bang) on the garage door and (6) _____ (invite) Colin to appear in one of the concerts he (7) _____ (organise) that year. Colin, however, (8) _____ (not accept) Leaf's invitation, because at that time he (9) _____ (prepare) for some important school exams.

Colin (10) _____ (pass) his exams and (11) _____ (go) to university to study engineering. At university he (12) _____ (meet) Kim O'Malley, who (13) _____ (study) chemistry. Kim played the saxophone. Being students, they (14) _____ (not have) much money and they usually (15) _____ (work) as waiters at weekends.

One evening in April 2008, while Colin and Kim (16) _____ (serve) customers, the manager (17) _____ (announce) that there would be no live music in the restaurant that night as the regular band could not come. Colin and Kim (18) _____ (persuade) the manager to let them play. All the customers and staff (19) _____ (be) amazed to hear how good their music (20) _____ (be). In the next six months Colin and Kim (21) _____ (earn) so much money they (22) _____ (decide) to leave university and go on tour. Their success has continued ever since.

17 Complete the first sentence with the verb in the past continuous. Write a second sentence with the verb in the past simple to say what happened next. Use your own ideas.

1 When my phone rang, I _was watching TV._
   I answered it but it was a wrong number.

2 I _____ when it started to rain.

3 Everyone _____ when the lights went out.

4 When we came out of the cinema, the sun _____

Present and past
(**I do / I am doing** and **I did / I was doing**)

Units 1–6, 17

18 Choose the correct alternative.

ADAM: Hello, Mike. What (1) <u>are you doing / do you do</u> in my part of London?
MIKE: Well, actually, (2) <u>I'm looking / I look</u> at these new flats (3) <u>they're building / they build</u> down the road here.
ADAM: Well, (4) <u>they're looking / they look</u> quite cool, but (5) <u>I'm thinking / I think</u> they're quite expensive. So (6) <u>are you wanting / do you want</u> to move to this area?
MIKE: Yes. In fact, well, the news is that Mandy and I (7) <u>are getting / get</u> married.
ADAM: Oh, wow! Congratulations. When (8) <u>were you deciding / did you decide</u>?
MIKE: Only last week. It was while (9) <u>we were staying / we stayed</u> with her family in Scotland. Now (10) <u>we try / we're trying</u> to find a suitable flat.
ADAM: I hope you manage to buy one of these.
MIKE: Oh, (11) <u>we aren't looking / we don't look</u> for one to buy. (12) <u>We aren't having / We don't have</u> enough money yet. (13) <u>We're wanting / We want</u> to rent one.
ADAM: Yes, of course. That's what Anna and I (14) <u>did / were doing</u> at first. After that, my brother (15) <u>was lending / lent</u> us some money. That's how (16) <u>we were managing / we managed</u> to buy ours.
MIKE: You're right. We must talk to our families before (17) <u>we choose / we're choosing</u> a flat.
ADAM: Yeah, my family (18) <u>gave / were giving</u> us a lot of help and advice. Now, what about a sandwich at my place? It's just round the corner.
MIKE: Oh yes, thanks. (19) <u>I looked / I was looking</u> for somewhere to eat when (20) <u>I was bumping / I bumped</u> into you.

19 Put the verbs into the correct form: present simple, present continuous, past simple or past continuous.

1 I remember the day you got engaged. I ....*was having*.... a shower when you phoned. (have)
2 He tried to explain his problems to his parents, but they just .... what he was talking about. (not / understand)
3 What have you put in my burger? It .... absolutely disgusting. (taste)
4 Mick always claimed that he was innocent, but for many years no-one .... him. (believe)
5 It's a great jacket, I know, but unfortunately it .... to me. I'm just borrowing it for the party this evening. (not / belong)
6 Why .... that thin dress? You'll freeze to death in this cold wind! (you / wear)
7 Zoe's fed up because she hurt her ankle when she .... this morning. (jog)
8 While I was admiring the view, someone .... my phone from my bag. (steal)
9 Look! .... that man standing at the checkout? I'm sure I know him. (you / see)
10 Tea or coffee? I'm making both, so just say which you .... (prefer)

Present and past

Units 1–6, 17

20

There are mistakes in eight of these sentences. Correct the sentences where necessary. Write 'OK' if the sentence is already correct.

1 The coffee is smelling wonderful. — The coffee smells wonderful.
2 Last year we visited Australia. — OK
3 The ship sank because the engineer wasn't calling for help until it was too late.
4 The reason I get fat is that I'm always tasting things while I'm cooking.
5 How is Jennifer? Does her health improve?
6 You're quite right, I'm completely agreeing with you.
7 What did you after you left school?
8 Now I understand what you're trying to say!
9 I can't imagine why you were believing all those stories.
10 Martin looked forward to a quiet evening when his brother came home from the football match with ten friends.
11 Philippa heard the election result as she was driving to work, so she phoned me when she got there.
12 I'm sorry, I've spilt your drink. Where are you keeping the paper towels?

21

Complete the email with suitable verbs in the correct form: present simple, present continuous, past simple or past continuous.

From: Alice
To: Anita
Subject: Hi

Hi Anita,

Thanks for the text you (1) ...sent... yesterday. I (2) .... to feel better now although my back still (3) .... if I (4) .... too far.

Last night I (5) .... some friends who (6) .... dinner near here. I (7) .... to the cafe quite easily, but while I (8) .... home, my back (9) .... to ache really badly. So today I (10) .... more careful.

It's great that you (11) .... to find that website about Indian music that you (12) .... for. I've got some DVDs if you (13) .... to borrow them.

I must lie down now because my back (14) .... to hurt again. Come and see me soon. I'm OK, but you know me, I (15) .... bored very quickly!

Love, Alice

Present and past

Units 1–6, 17

22 Complete the questions with suitable verbs in the correct form: present simple, present continuous, past simple or past continuous.

1. Why **are you wearing** your coat and hat? — I'm really cold.
2. How often .... your teeth? — Twice a day.
3. When .... your driving test? — Last Friday. Would you like a lift somewhere?
4. .... this programme? — No, it's not very interesting.
5. What time .... to bed last night? — About one o'clock I think.
6. .... this jumper is too small for me? — Not at all. It's fine.
7. What .... at one o'clock this morning? — I was at home watching TV.
8. What time .... ? — Nine o'clock usually.

English Grammar in Use Supplementary Exercises

Present perfect simple and continuous
(I have done and I have been doing)

Units 7–12

23 Complete the email with the present perfect simple form of the verbs.

From: Theresa
To: Flora
Subject: Hi

Hi Flora
As you can see, I (1) _'ve arrived_ (arrive) safely. Paul and I (2) .... (already / do) lots of things even though (3) .... (I / only / be) in New York twenty-four hours. (4) .... (I / not sleep) for two days! (5) .... (I / take) about a hundred photos already. Paul (6) .... (show) me lots of famous landmarks and (7) .... (I / eat) a real American breakfast. (8) .... (I / ride) in a yellow cab and (9) .... (I / travel) on the subway too. (10) .... (I / not spend) any money yet because Paul (11) .... (pay) for everything so far. I'll email you some more photos when (12) .... (I / have) some sleep.
Love Theresa

1 attachment

24 Tick (✓) the sentence which means the same as the first sentence.

1 Have you ever visited Ibiza?
 a Did you visit Ibiza?
 b Have you been to Ibiza? ✓
 c Have you visited Ibiza recently?

2 This is the first time I've been skiing.
 a I've been skiing once before.
 b I haven't been skiing for a long time.
 c I've never been skiing before.

3 I've had two holidays this year.
 a I've just come back from holiday.
 b I've been on holiday twice this year.
 c I've been away for two weeks.

4 We've just got home from the beach.
 a We were at the beach very recently.
 b We haven't been to the beach for a long time.
 c We went to the beach yesterday.

5 My manager hasn't been at work for a week.
 a My manager has left the company.
 b My manager has been away for a week.
 c My manager didn't come to work last week.

6 I haven't checked my emails since this morning.
 a I have just checked my emails.
 b I haven't checked my emails today.
 c I checked my emails this morning.

Present perfect simple and continuous

Units 7–12

25

Complete the conversation with the verbs from the box in the correct form: present perfect simple or present perfect continuous. In some cases both forms are possible. You need to use some of the verbs more than once. Read the whole conversation before you begin.

> be   come   do   drive   find   have   look

Jane is being interviewed by Nicola for a job working with young children.

NICOLA: Come in, Jane. Please sit down. Would you like a coffee?

JANE: Thank you, actually I (1) **'ve just had** (just) one.

NICOLA: Oh good. Now, do you know this area at all?

JANE: Quite well. I've got friends who live in this town, so I (2) .... here for holidays since I was a child. I'm staying with them at the moment, actually.

NICOLA: Oh, that's nice. And do you have a driving licence?

JANE: Yes. I (3) .... for four years now.

NICOLA: And would you say you're a careful driver?

JANE: Yes, I think so. At least I (4) .... (never) an accident.

NICOLA: Good. Now, could you tell me why you think you would be right for this job?

JANE: Well, I (5) .... (always) interested in working with small children. And I (6) .... two holiday jobs looking after children.

NICOLA: How do you think you would cope in an emergency?

JANE: I'm quite a calm person, I think. I (7) .... a first aid course too. I got a certificate.

NICOLA: That's good. Now, this job isn't permanent, as you know. We need someone for about a year. How would that fit with your long-term plans?

JANE: I'd like to work abroad eventually. But I want some full-time experience first. I (8) .... a Nursery Teacher's course this year. We finish next week, in fact.

NICOLA: When would you be able to start?

JANE: As soon as I finish my course.

NICOLA: Excellent. And would you live with your friends?

JANE: Well, probably not. I want to rent a small flat. I (9) .... in the paper every day, but I (10) .... (not) anything yet.

NICOLA: Well, if you get the job, we'll try to help you. Now, would you like to come and meet some of the children?

JANE: Oh, yes.

NICOLA: Right, if you'll just follow me then.

Present perfect simple and continuous

Units 7–12

26
Tick (✓) the sentences which are correct. In some pairs, one sentence is correct. In other pairs, both sentences are correct.

1. She's had a headache all day. ✓ — She's been having a headache all day.
2. I've wanted a cat for a long time. — I've been wanting a cat for a long time.
3. They've eaten lunch. — They've been eating lunch.
4. I've known her for two years. — I've been knowing her for two years.
5. He's been very helpful. — He's been being very helpful.
6. He's tasted the soup. — He's been tasting the soup.
7. They've seen this movie before. — They've been seeing this movie before.
8. I've seen a throat specialist. — I've been seeing a throat specialist.
9. We've realised where we are now. — We've been realising where we are now.
10. It's belonged to us for many years. — It's been belonging to us for many years.
11. He's explained the plan to us. — He's been explaining the plan to us.
12. You've broken my phone! — You've been breaking my phone!

27
Put the verbs into the correct form: present perfect simple or present perfect continuous.

1. John's terribly upset. *He's broken off* (he / break off) his engagement to Megan. Apparently *she's been seeing* (she / see) someone else while *he's been* (he / be) in Africa.
2. Could you translate this Arabic song for me? I understood Arabic when I was a child, but .... (I / forget) it all.
3. What's that mark on the side of the car? .... (you / have) an accident?
4. The lock on this case is broken. .... (you / play about) with it?
5. Your Portuguese is very good. .... (you / study) it long?
6. Of course you don't know what I think! .... (you / never / ask) my opinion.
7. I'm not surprised .... (he / fail) the exam. .... (he / not / work) hard recently.
8. Mina's hands are very dirty. .... (she / repair) her bike.
9. I'm going to make some lunch for the kids. .... (they / swim) all morning. I'm sure they're hungry.
10. .... (I / do) grammar exercises all morning. I deserve a break.
11. Where's my phone? This is the third time .... (I / lose) it today!
12. Oh, do be quiet. .... (you / grumble) all weekend!
13. Since Maria won that talent show .... (she / spend) money like water. .... (she / buy) a new car and .... (she / move) to a big new house. .... (she / give) wonderful parties every weekend too. In fact, I'm going to one tomorrow.

Present perfect simple and continuous

Units 7–12

28 Complete the sentences with the verbs in the correct form: present perfect simple or present perfect continuous.

1. earlier this morning / now
   – You look very tired.
   – Yes, I am. I've been cleaning my room all morning.

2. a moment ago / now
   – Why do you need a new camera?
   – Because I ....

3. earlier this afternoon / now
   – How did you get in such a mess?
   – Well, I .... sausages.

4. earlier this year / now
   – You dance much better than you used to!
   – Thank you. Actually, I ....

5. about now / now
   – Isn't your brother here?
   – Sorry, no. He ....

6. earlier / now
   – You're looking very nice.
   – Thanks, I ....

7. a few minutes ago / now
   – Why are you crying?
   – Don't worry. It's because I ....

8. earlier this week / now
   – Can you give me a lift to work?
   – I'm afraid I can't. You see, I ....

Present perfect simple and continuous; past simple

(**I have done** and **I have been doing**; **I did**)

Units 5, 7–14

29 Complete the second sentence so that it has a similar meaning to the first sentence.

1. We haven't been to a beach party for over a year.
   The last time we *went to a beach party* was over a year ago.
2. Your wedding was the last time I wore a long dress.
   I .... since your wedding.
3. It's nearly twenty years since my father saw his brother.
   My father .... for nearly twenty years.
4. James went to Bratislava last Friday and is still there.
   James has .... to Bratislava.
5. When did you learn to drive?
   How long is it .... to drive?
6. The last time I went scuba diving was when we were in Egypt.
   I haven't .... we were in Egypt.
7. You haven't topped up your phone for weeks.
   It's weeks .... your phone.
8. We started looking for a flat two months ago and we're still looking.
   We've .... a flat for two months.
9. This is the first time I've been to a nightclub.
   I .... to a nightclub before.
10. Kim lost her job a year ago and is still trying to find one.
    Kim .... a job for a whole year.

30 Use your own ideas to complete the sentences. Use the present perfect simple, the present perfect continuous or the past simple.

1. Since we bought this car, *we've done lots of trips round the country.*
   or *we've been doing lots of trips round the country.*
2. *My colleague was ill, so I had to work overtime* last week.
3. .... for several years.
4. .... since yesterday.
5. When I was a child, ...
6. .... ten minutes ago.
7. It's three weeks since ....
8. For the past three weeks ....
9. .... in 2010.
10. .... since I came into this room.
11. Last December ....
12. .... since I got up this morning.

Present perfect and present
(I have done / I have been doing and I do / I am doing)

Units 1–4, 7–12

31 Choose the correct alternative.

Megan meets her friend Jess in a cafe.

MEGAN: Hi, Jess, how are you? (1) I haven't seen / I haven't been seeing you since the summer.

JESS: No, (2) I've been revising / I've revised for my exams. They're next week. What about you?

MEGAN: Well, a few days ago I met a website designer, Steve, (3) who's looking / who's been looking for some help for weeks. (4) He offers / He's offered me some work from next week.

JESS: That's great.

MEGAN: Yeah, and every day since then (5) I look / I've been looking at his sites. (6) He's designed / He's been designing three or four really cool ones already. But (7) he doesn't have / he isn't having enough time to do all the new ones. That's why (8) he's needing / he needs me.

JESS: That's really good. Hey, who's that guy over there? (9) He's looked / He's been looking at us since we met.

MEGAN: Oh, wow, that's Steve, the guy (10) I've been telling / I tell you about.

JESS: (11) He's looking / He looks like a student or something.

MEGAN: Shh. (12) He's coming / He comes over.

STEVE: Hi, Megan.

MEGAN: Steve, this is my friend Jess.

STEVE: Hello. (13) Do you using / Are you using the Wi-Fi in here at the moment?

JESS: Yes. (14) I come / I'm coming here most days for lunch and since the cafe's got Wi-Fi (15) I've checked / I've been checking my email at the same time.

STEVE: And (16) do you enjoy / are you enjoying the food here?

JESS: Er, yes. It's always very good. But why?

STEVE: Oh, just interested. (17) I own / I'm owning this cafe.

MEGAN: I didn't know that!

Present perfect and present

Units 1–4, 7–12

32

Complete the sentences with the verbs from the box in the correct form: present perfect simple, present perfect continuous, present simple or present continuous.

| not / be | ~~deal~~ | ~~not / finish~~ | have | not / know | live | see | not / see |
| not / speak | stare | stay | suffer | wait | not / want | watch | |

1 I **haven't finished** checking the emails because I **'ve been dealing** with customers all morning.
2 Thank you, but I really .... any more juice. I .... two large glasses already.
3 Paul .... from earache since the weekend.
   He .... the doctor twice, but it's still not better.
4 We .... why Sara is upset, but she .... to us for ages.
5 Why .... you .... at me like that?
   I suppose you .... a woman on a motorbike before!
6 I .... with my cousin in London for a few days.
   I .... here before, but he .... here for several years, so he can show me around.
7 I'm sorry I'm late. .... you .... a long time?
8 We .... this stupid film since lunchtime. Let's switch over to the other channel.

33

Complete the email with suitable verbs in the correct form: present perfect simple, present perfect continuous, present simple or present continuous.

Dear Nick,
We (1) **'re having** a wonderful time here in Prague.
We (2) .... here for three days now
and we (3) .... to stay for the rest
of the week because we (4) ....
ourselves so much. We (5) .... the
Charles Bridge and the Castle, and this morning we
(6) .... around other historic places,
including Kafka's house. I (7) .... this
photo just before lunch. We (8) ....
any souvenirs yet, but we (9) ....
some good art galleries
and shops. Fortunately, the weather (10) .... too cold so far.
People (11) .... it can be really bad at this time of year and of
course it often (12) .... heavily here! As this is the first time
we (13) .... to Prague, we (14) .... that we're
just lucky.
See you soon,
Roberto and Jan

Present perfect and present

Units 1–4, 7–12

34 Put the verbs into the correct form: present perfect simple, present perfect continuous, present simple or present continuous.

Sam is the captain of his local football team. He's talking to his brother, Dave.

SAM: Dave, I'm worried about the team.
DAVE: But why? (1) *You've won* (You / win) every game this season.
SAM: Yeah, (2) .... (we / be) very lucky.
That's (3) .... (what / cause) me problems now.
DAVE: How come?
SAM: Well, (4) .... (we / practise) twice a week since the beginning of this season and (5) .... (that / really / make) a difference. Now, some of the guys say that's not necessary because (6) .... (we / always / win). The thing is, I'm afraid that if (7) .... (we / not / practise) so often, we may start losing matches. Like, (8) .... (we / play) Donnington on Saturday and (9) .... (everyone / agree) they're a really strong team. The trouble is, (10) .... (we / not / practise) since Monday.
DAVE: I can see (11) .... (you / have) a problem. What can you do?
SAM: I think the problem is really Callum.
DAVE: The big guy (12) .... (who / play) for you since last season?
SAM: Yeah, and (13) .... (he / usually / score) most of the goals. The trouble is, since the summer (14) .... (he / arrive) for training really late. And now some of the others (15) .... (begin) to do the same. When I try to talk to him, (16) .... (he / refuse) to listen to what (17) .... (I / say).
DAVE: Well, you're the captain, tell him he can't play if (18) .... (he / not / listen) to you.
SAM: OK, but (19) .... (I / not / like) it. What if he gets angry and leaves the team?
DAVE: I'm sure he won't.
SAM: Yeah, well. (20) .... (I / hope) not.

Present perfect, present and past
(I have done / I have been doing, I do / I am doing and I did)

Units 1–5, 7–12

35 There are seven mistakes in this email. Correct the mistakes.

> From: mariannanov@wtmail.com
> To: maaziz@market.solutions.co.uk
> Subject: Temporary manager
>
> Dear Mr Aziz,
>
> I would like to apply for the job of temporary manager which <u>I see</u> advertised on your website. *[I have seen]*
>
> I am twenty years old. I was born in Poland, but my family moved to England when I was twelve and I am living here ever since. I left school since three years and since then I am having several jobs in tourism and marketing. For the past six months I am working for Go-Places Agency. The manager has been saying that he is willing to give me a reference.
>
> I speak Polish and English fluently. I have also learnt Spanish since I left school, so I speak some Spanish too.
>
> I hope you will consider my application.
>
> Yours sincerely,
> Marianna Nowak

36 Write an email applying for this job. You may write for yourself or you may invent an applicant.

> **Student jobsearch**   Temporary jobs
>
> **Assistant shop manager – Allingham**
>
> Busy souvenir shop seeks bright, helpful person for two months in summer.
> Must speak fluent English in addition to at least one other language. Experience and qualifications not essential, but desirable. Good pay and conditions.
> Email giving details + one referee to Nicole.Sparks@studentjobsearch.co.uk

> To: Nicole.Sparks@studentjobsearch.co.uk
> Subject: Assistant shop manager

Present perfect and past simple
(I have done / I have been doing and I did)

Units 13–14

37 Match the beginning of each sentence with the most suitable ending to make a story.

1 The Ocean Hotel opened	a half an hour ago.	1 .....c.....
2 There's been a nightclub there	b last night.	2 ....
3 I went clubbing there	c ~~in 2008.~~	3 ....
4 I lost my coat	d since January.	4 ....
5 I phoned the club	e all day.	5 ....
6 The manager asked me to wait	f when I went there.	6 ....
7 That's why I've felt cold	g for a few days in case it's found.	7 ....

38 Choose the correct alternative.

1 My sister <u>has been</u> / ~~was~~ interested in medicine ever since <u>she has been</u> / <u>she was</u> a child.
2 How long <u>have you studied / did you study</u> before <u>you have qualified / you qualified</u>?
3 Where <u>have you first met / did you first meet</u> your boyfriend?
4 Is this the first time <u>you've cooked / you cooked</u> pasta?
5 <u>We've wanted / We wanted</u> to go to out last night, but <u>we haven't had / we didn't have</u> any money.
6 What can we do? I'm sure something <u>has happened / happened</u> to Alex. <u>We've been texting / We texted</u> him for over an hour and <u>he still hasn't replied / he still hasn't been replying</u>.
7 <u>We have posted / We posted</u> the new DVD to you three weeks ago. If <u>you haven't received / you didn't receive</u> it yet, please email us immediately.
8 I'm exhausted because <u>I've worked / I've been working</u> in a restaurant for the past three weeks. <u>I've never realised / I never realised</u> before how hard the work is!

39 Complete the sentences with the verbs from the box in the correct form: present perfect or past simple.

~~be~~	be	break	earn	forget	give
go	have	offer	phone	tell	train

1 Bill _has been_ off work all this week.
2 Gina .... to the cinema every weekend when she was a student.
3 Pippa .... very quiet recently. Is she OK?
4 Eric .... every day for six months before he ran the marathon.
5 How long .... Neil .... his present job?
6 .... Tina .... her parents since she left home?
7 Ow, that hurt! I think I .... my toe.
8 Jock .... me about his problems last night.
9 I .... Sue's mobile number. Do you have it?
10 Jane .... more money in her last job, but she enjoys this one more.
11 .... Mark .... you his address before he left?
12 My brother .... to lend me his car tomorrow, so I needn't get the bus.

Present perfect and past simple — Units 13–14

40 Put the verbs into the correct form: present perfect simple or past simple. Read the whole text before you begin.

Then and Now

Twenty years ago only a few people (1) _realised_ (realise) how greatly technology was about to transform our daily lives. This short period of time (2) _____ (see) enormous changes in how we live, study and work.

Trips to the supermarket which once (3) _____ (take) half the weekend have been replaced with online ordering. Music lovers who a decade ago (4) _____ (spend) hours wandering around shops, simply download the tracks they want to hear. Information which (5) _____ (require) hours of research in a library (6) _____ (become) available to anybody in a few clicks on the keyboard. The spread of laptops and WiFi (7) _____ (enable) students and business people to work almost anywhere at anytime and mobile phones (8) _____ (transform) the way people organise their lives.

Some of us may wonder, however, how much our lives (9) _____ (improve) in recent years. Online banking, for example, (10) _____ (replace) the friendly bank clerk who (11) _____ (know) your name with an impersonal website. Teachers complain that students (12) _____ (learn) to copy and paste instead of thinking for themselves. There are fears that governments (13) _____ (not/do) enough to safeguard personal data held on computers. Certainly, many people may now be wondering whether modern technology (14) _____ (bring) us as many problems as it (15) _____ (solve).

Present perfect and past simple

Units 13–14

41 Alex wants to go to an art college and is being interviewed by Tom Smith, one of the lecturers. Complete the questions which Tom asks him. Read the whole conversation before you begin.

TOM: Right, Alex, let's find out something about you. When (1) *did you leave* school?
ALEX: Five years ago, actually.
TOM: And where (2) .... since then?
ALEX: Well, I've had several jobs.
TOM: What (3) .... first?
ALEX: I worked in a cafe for about a year. I needed to save a lot of money.
TOM: Why (4) .... the money?
ALEX: I wanted to travel a bit before I started studying.
TOM: Where (5) .... to go?
ALEX: Well, the Middle East, Latin America, Australia …
TOM: Wow! And (6) .... all those places?
ALEX: No, not yet. I've been to Brazil and Peru so far. And I spent some months in Turkey.
TOM: Where (7) .... there?
ALEX: With some friends near Izmir. It was great.
TOM: You're very lucky. And now you want to come to college.
 (8) .... some work to show me?
ALEX: Um, yes, I've got some paintings here.
TOM: Where (9) .... these?
ALEX: Mostly in Turkey.
TOM: (10) .... anything in South America?
ALEX: No, I didn't have time really. And I was travelling light, so I just did some pencil sketches. They're behind the paintings.
TOM: Well, Alex, I'm very impressed. When (11) .... interested in painting and drawing?
ALEX: I think I always have been.
TOM: I can believe that. This work is very good.
ALEX: Thank you very much.

Present perfect and past simple

Units 13–14

42 Choose ten of the pictures and write true sentences about yourself. Use the present perfect or past simple.

do / washing up	drive / car	eat / noodles	wear / hat	ride / motorbike
get / married	play / computer game	play / golf	pass / exam	break / leg
watch / TV	ride / bike	study / English	drink / milk	text / my best friend

1 I *haven't played a computer game* .... since last month.
2 Yesterday I ....
3 In the past six months I ....
4 Since my last birthday I ....
5 I .... recently.
6 Last year I ....
7 Six months ago I ....
8 I .... since I was a child.
9 I .... yesterday evening.
10 This week I ....

26 *English Grammar in Use Supplementary Exercises*

Past simple, past continuous and past perfect
(I did, I was doing and I had done / I had been doing)

Units 5–6, 15–16

43
Choose the correct alternative.

From: Nonna@zapnet.com
To: GHL@zapnet.com
Cc: Margo35@kwikmail.co.uk
Subject: INTERNATIONAL STUDENT CONFERENCE

Hi!
Thought you'd like to know that the conference was very successful. 🙂 The talks (1) <u>were / had been</u> really interesting and all the speakers (2) <u>had prepared / prepared</u> their material very thoroughly. Everyone agreed we should do the same next year.

However there were some problems with the conference centre. 🙁 When we (3) <u>arrived / had arrived</u>, we (4) <u>discovered / had discovered</u> that the manager (5) <u>reserved / had reserved</u> the wrong room for us. This meant that we (6) <u>didn't have / hadn't had</u> enough space. Unfortunately, he couldn't let us have the larger room because he (7) <u>gave / had given</u> it to another group, which was even bigger than ours. 🙁🙁

He (8) <u>also misunderstood / had also misunderstood</u> the letter explaining what food we (9) <u>wanted / had wanted</u>. In fact, we (10) <u>suspected / had suspected</u> that he (11) <u>lost / had lost</u> it. I don't recommend using that place again!

CU
Nonna

44
There are mistakes in all of these sentences. Correct the sentences.

1 I was pleased to see my friends from uni at the conference last week <u>as we didn't see each other</u> since graduation. — *as we hadn't seen each other*

2 By the time we reached the stadium, the match ended and the spectators were leaving.

3 At the end of the meal, he found he couldn't pay his share of the bill because he didn't bring his wallet with him.

4 We were pleased that Gary was having his laptop with him, but we were less pleased when we discovered that he hadn't charged the battery.

5 When I came out of the cinema, I had found that a thief had taken my phone from my bag.

6 At first the authorities thought the athlete had been using drugs, but they soon realised the lab mixed up the test results.

7 When my cousin came into the room, I didn't recognise him because I didn't see him since he was at primary school.

8 We couldn't find anywhere central to stay when we arrived in Rome, so we had decided to book a hotel room the next time.

English Grammar in Use Supplementary Exercises

Past simple, past continuous and past perfect

Units 5–6, 15–16

45 Complete the sentences with suitable verbs in the correct form: past perfect simple or past perfect continuous.

1. Why did Vicki have a shower? — Because *she'd been working out*.
2. Why did Becca give you flowers? — Because she ....
3. Why didn't Jordan answer the door? — Because he ....
4. Why didn't Simon arrive for his interview? — Because he ....
5. Why didn't Alex eat any lunch? — Because he ....
6. Why did Cora miss the bus? — Because she ....
7. Why didn't Ellie go to the beach? — Because she ....
8. Why did Chris lose his job? — Because he ....

Past simple, past continuous and past perfect

Units 5–6, 15–16

46

Put the verbs into the correct form: past simple, past continuous, past perfect simple or past perfect continuous.

Kylie has called to see her boyfriend Gary. They are both angry.

GARY: Kylie, I'm surprised to see you.
KYLIE: Yeah? Well, I think you owe me an explanation.
GARY: What about you? (1) _I saw_ (I / see) you in the cafe last night.
(2) _____ (We / arrange) to meet at the cinema, if you remember.
KYLIE: So why (3) _____ (you / not / come) into the cafe if you saw me?
GARY: (4) _____ (I / be) too angry. And cold.
(5) _____ (I / wait) outside the cinema for three-quarters of an hour.
KYLIE: But why? (6) _____ (you / not / get) my text?
GARY: What text?
KYLIE: The text (7) _____ (I / send) you yesterday afternoon.
GARY: What are you talking about?
KYLIE: (8) _____ (I / walk) past the cinema yesterday lunchtime when (9) _____ (I / notice) that (10) _____ (they / change) the movie. So (11) _____ (I / text) you to tell you.
GARY: (12) _____ (I / not / get) any texts from you yesterday.
KYLIE: What? Let me look at your phone. Yes, it's here.
GARY: Oh, no! Of course, my phone wasn't charged yesterday. I'm so sorry I was angry. It's just that, well, while (13) _____ (I / wait), (14) _____ (I / worry) about (15) _____ (what / happen) to you. Then (16) _____ (I / see) you in the cafe. (17) _____ (You / laugh) with your friends and (18) _____ (I / realise) that (19) _____ (you / sit) there in the warm with them all evening. That's why (20) _____ (I / lose) my temper.
KYLIE: Never mind. Let's forget it. Where shall we go now?
GARY: What's on at the cinema, then?
KYLIE: A new musical. (21) _____ (My sister / see) it at the weekend. (22) _____ (She / sing) the theme song all day yesterday.
GARY: Oh, you must be tired of hearing it.
KYLIE: I am. Let's just go and have something to eat, shall we?
GARY: Yes, that's a good idea.

Past simple, past continuous and used to
(**I did**, **I was doing** and **I used to do**)

Units 5–6, 18

47
Write sentences with **used to** or **didn't use to** and the verbs provided.

1 I had a yacht, but I sold it when my business failed. (own)
   I used to own a yacht.

2 I often eat olives now, although I wasn't keen on them when I was younger. (like)

3 I seem to have lost interest in meeting new people. (enjoy)

4 My sister has started visiting art galleries since moving to Paris. (be interested)

5 Now that I'm married, I have less time for football. (play)

6 My brother had his hair cut short when he left college. (have)

7 I didn't really see my uncle until he bought a house near ours. (live)

8 My husband had a job in Beijing before we lived here. (work)

9 I retired from the university five years ago. (teach)

10 We've bought bikes since we moved to the countryside. (cycle)

48
Choose the correct alternative.

It is sometimes said that there is nothing new in the world of fashion. Annabelle was a well-known model during the seventies. When her granddaughter Zoe was a schoolchild, she (1) ~~was enjoying~~ / <u>used to enjoy</u> looking at granny's old photo albums. She (2) <u>was finding / found</u> it hard to believe that granny (3) <u>was wearing / used to wear</u> such strange clothes.
(4) <u>Did people really use to think / Were people really thinking</u> flared trousers looked good? And those ugly platform shoes! Annabelle (5) <u>was admitting / admitted</u> that people
(6) <u>were often falling / often used to fall</u> over because their heels were so high.
When Zoe went to university, however, Annabelle noticed to her amusement that seventies styles (7) <u>were / used to be</u> in fashion again. 'I (8) <u>planned / was planning</u> to throw all my old clothes away,' she said, 'but Zoe went to a party last week, and guess what she (9) <u>used to wear / was wearing</u> – that's right, some of my old clothes!'

Past simple, past continuous and used to

Units 5–6, 18

49 Underline the verbs which can be changed to used to (used to work / used to play / used to be, etc.) instead of the past simple. If no change is possible, write 'No change'. Rewrite the sentences with used to where possible.

1 In the winter vacation, Dan <u>worked</u> in a cafe while his friends were skiing.
   In the winter vacation, Dan used to work in a cafe while his friends were skiing.

2 Bruce cycled from Naples to Athens last summer, stopping each night in a different town.
   No change.

3 My girlfriend had a favourite handbag which she had bought with her first wages.

4 As Lynda was getting out of the boat, her foot slipped and she fell into the river.

5 Before the new shopping centre was built, there was a football stadium here.

6 Jasper complained that the street wasn't full of litter until the fast food restaurant opened.

7 During our cruise I took several photos of the seabirds which followed the ship.

8 While I was waiting for the bus, I noticed a group of tourists who were listening to a guide.

9 The music in this club was very boring before they installed a new sound system.

10 I spent a lot of time helping with the housework when I was a kid, but my sister didn't help at all.

11 The politicians made lots of promises before the election but kept none of them, as usual.

50 Write true sentences about yourself with used to or didn't use to and the words from the box.

| cinema | friends | grandparents | homework |
| jeans | music | restaurants | television |

1 I used to go on holiday with my parents, but now I go with my friends.
2 I didn't use to wear jeans when I was a child.
3
4
5
6
7
8

Past simple, past continuous and used to

Units 5–6, 18

51 Complete the sentences with suitable verbs in the correct form: past simple, past continuous or **used to**.

1. When did Ellie meet her boyfriend?
   I think it was while she **was studying** in the States.

2. Why does Warren keep shouting at people?
   I don't know. He .... so bad-tempered.

3. How long is it since you .... a holiday?
   Not since last year.

4. Is the club shut already?
   Yeah, it .... open much later than it does now.

5. What was that text you just sent?
   I .... some cinema tickets for tomorrow night.

6. Have you ever ridden a motorbike?
   Yes, once. But I .... off at a roundabout.

7. Oh, I .... it while I .... in Rome.
   I didn't know you understood Italian!

8. How do you know London so well?
   Well, I .... here.

Present, present perfect and past

Units 1–18

52 Choose the correct alternative.

A PETE: Whereabouts in Brighton (1) ~~do you live~~ / did you live / ~~have you lived~~ when
(2) you were / you've been / you were being a child?

PATRICK: The part called Kemp Town. (3) Do you know / Did you know / Have you known it?

PETE: Oh, yes. (4) I was eating / I used to eat / I've eaten there most weekends when
(5) I was doing / I've been doing / I've done my degree at the university.

B HELEN: When (6) are you hearing / did you hear / have you heard the result of your law exam?

CLARA: When (7) I phoned / I've phoned / I'd phoned my boss. (8) She's checking / She's been checking / She was checking the results online when (9) I'd rung / I rang / I was ringing, so (10) she's told / she was telling / she told me then.

HELEN: (11) Do you expect / Have you expected / Had you been expecting to do so well?

CLARA: Not really, to be honest!

HELEN: (12) Are you texting / Do you text / Have you texted your husband yet?

CLARA: Not yet.

HELEN: Go on! (13) He waited / He's waited / He's been waiting to hear from you all day.

53 Put the verbs into the correct form: present simple, present continuous, past simple, past continuous, present perfect simple, present perfect continuous or past perfect simple.

1. Tom has started training regularly since he ...*joined*... (join) the gym.
2. How often .... (you / visit) your cousins when .... (you / be) in Singapore last year?
3. I .... (not top up) my phone credit yet. How much .... (you / think) I need for a month?
4. The filling station manager called the police when he .... (realise) that someone .... (drive) off without paying for their petrol.
5. Sharon's health .... (seem) much better these days than it used to be. Perhaps she .... (take) vitamins as the doctor .... (advise).
6. Eddie .... (set) fire to his kitchen last week when he .... (fry) sausages. He .... (sort out) the mess ever since, as you can imagine.
7. My grandmother was a wonderful woman. She .... (spend) most of her life teaching adults who .... (miss) the opportunity to go to school when they .... (be) children.
8. I .... (always / want) to visit Japan. Now that I .... (have) the chance, I .... (decide) to take it.
9. We .... (arrive) at the music festival on Friday afternoon, but a lot of people .... (get) there in the morning and the queue for tickets .... (be) already long.
10. My sister's in Vietnam at the moment. She .... (have) such a great time she .... (want) to stay another six months.

English Grammar in Use Supplementary Exercises

The future: present tenses and will/shall
(I do / I am doing and I will/shall do)

Units 19, 21–22

54 Choose the correct alternative.

A BEN: Are you busy at the moment, Sam?
SAM: Yes. (1) ~~I prepare~~ / I'm preparing for a conference next Wednesday, but (2) that only lasts / that is only lasting until Friday so I'm free after that.

B PAT: Oh dear, I've spilt my coffee.
ALAN: Don't worry! (3) I get / I'll get a cloth.

C WILL: What time (4) does your evening class finish / is your evening class finishing?
LIZ: Half past nine.
WILL: (5) Shall I come / Do I come and collect you?
LIZ: Thanks, but (6) I meet / I'm meeting my sister for a drink.

D MIKE: Mum, (7) will you talk / are you talking to Dad for me?
MUM: What's the problem?
MIKE: Last week he said I could use the car at the weekend, but now (8) he doesn't let / he won't let me after all. I need it to get to the match (9) I play / I'm playing on Sunday.
MUM: OK. (10) I try / I'll try to make him change his mind. I expect (11) he's agreeing / he'll agree when I explain.

55 Complete the email with the verbs from the box in the correct form: present simple, present continuous or will.

be   do   ~~go~~   include   let   see   work

Hi Milo

I've had an idea about next year's holiday. I (1) _'m going_ to the Far East on a tour, starting on 10th July. Would you like to come too?

I know you (2) _____ in Moscow next summer, but I'm sure your company (3) _____ you fly to the Far East instead of coming back to Europe.

The tour (4) _____ ancient sites in Vietnam, Cambodia and Malaysia. There (5) _____ chances to take a break and relax too. Have a look at their website www.tourfarther.com and let me know what you think quickly because I (6) _____ the travel agent on Monday. I hope we (7) _____ this tour together.

All the best
Pedro

The future: present tenses and will/shall

Units 19, 21–22

56
Put the verbs into the correct form: present simple, present continuous or the **will/shall** future.

Gina and Mickey are going to an international students' conference. Gina's checking with Mickey about the arrangements he's made for them.

GINA: Is everything arranged for tomorrow? What time (1) _does our plane leave_ (our plane / leave)?

MICKEY: At seven-thirty, so (2) .... (I / collect) you from your house at five.

GINA: Five! (3) .... (I / have to) get up in the middle of the night.

MICKEY: I'm sorry, but we must check in by six and I think (4) .... (there / probably / be) a long queue.

GINA: Oh, OK. What about the other end?

MICKEY: Well, (5) .... (a local student / come) to the airport to meet us. He texted me this morning.

GINA: That's good. (6) .... (We / be able to) talk to him on the way to the hostel.

MICKEY: Right. I believe (7) .... (the conference / not start) until late afternoon. Anyway, (8) .... (they / email) the programme to us before we leave.

GINA: Great. (9) .... (I / read) it on the plane, I expect. Now, I'd better go and pack.

MICKEY: Yeah, me too. See you tomorrow at six.

GINA: Oh, yeah. I hope (10) .... (I / be) awake.

MICKEY: So do I.

57
Complete the following sentences about yourself using the words in brackets.

1 This lesson _ends at twelve o'clock_ . (end)
2 At the weekend _I'll probably go to the cinema_ . (probably go)
3 Next summer .... (visit)
4 When I finish this exercise, ... (be)
5 Tomorrow evening I expect .... (eat)
6 At the end of my course .... (probably speak)
7 My next class .... (begin)
8 Next week .... (have)
9 My course .... (finish)

The future: present tenses and **will/shall**

Units 19, 21–22

58 Imagine that you are in the following situations. Write what you say using will, shall or won't.

1 YOU
You offer to help her.
You say: _I'll take the briefcase for you._
or _Shall I carry something?_

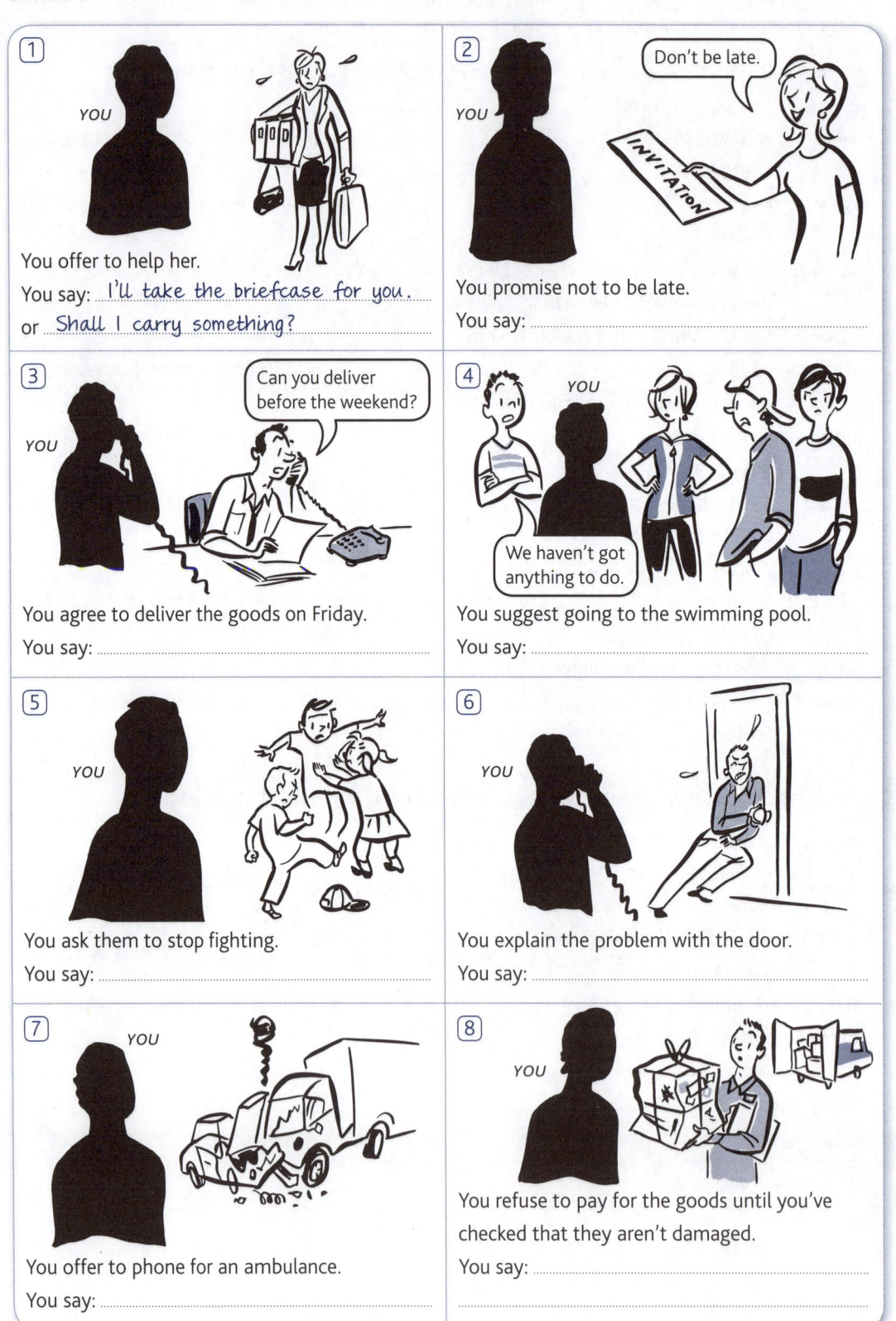

2 YOU — "Don't be late."
You promise not to be late.
You say: ....

3 YOU — "Can you deliver before the weekend?"
You agree to deliver the goods on Friday.
You say: ....

4 YOU — "We haven't got anything to do."
You suggest going to the swimming pool.
You say: ....

5 YOU
You ask them to stop fighting.
You say: ....

6 YOU
You explain the problem with the door.
You say: ....

7 YOU
You offer to phone for an ambulance.
You say: ....

8 YOU
You refuse to pay for the goods until you've checked that they aren't damaged.
You say: ....

The future: present continuous, will/shall, going to
(**I am doing**, **I will/shall do** and **I am going to do**)

Units 19–23

59
Write sentences with **going to** and the words in brackets.

1 It's Rowland's birthday next week. (send him a card)
   I'm going to send him a card

2 Look at those dark clouds. (rain very soon)

3 John forgot his Mum's birthday. (be in trouble)

4 This room is a mess. (who / help me tidy up?)

5 Alex and Tony can't afford to stay in a hotel. (buy a tent)

6 This music is boring. (not come to this club again)

7 I need to get more exercise. (walk to work from now on)

8 I'm very tired this morning. (have another coffee)

9 We haven't got any money. (how / get home?)

10 I need to leave home very early tomorrow. (buy petrol tonight)

11 My parents dislike flying. (travel to Prague by train)

12 Leila's lost her phone. (contact her?)

60
Choose the correct alternative.

1 The sports club has put up the prices again. I'll cancel / **I'm going to cancel** my membership.
2 I've talked to my boss, but he's very unhelpful and won't do / isn't going to do anything about the problem.
3 I'll go / I'm going to go into town this afternoon. Can I get you anything?
4 Will you hold / Are you going to hold this box for a moment while I unpack it?
5 I hear the government's announced they'll raise / they're going to raise taxes again.
6 My car won't start / isn't going to start. It must be the cold, I think.
7 I'll start / I'm going to start a new job next week.
8 I'm so sorry I forgot your birthday. Why don't you come round tomorrow evening and I'll cook / I'm going to cook you a meal?
9 I took these trousers back to the shop, but they won't change / aren't going to change them without a receipt.
10 You look tired. Shall we eat / Are we going to eat early this evening?
11 John's sold his car. He'll buy / He's going to buy a bike, he says.
12 I've decided what to do for my holiday. I'll go / I'm going to go to Morocco.

English Grammar in Use Supplementary Exercises

The future: present continuous, **will/shall**, going to

Units 19–23

61 Put the verbs into the correct form: the **will/shall** future or the **going to** future.

Mary and Nigel run a sportswear shop together. They are having money problems.

Monday

MARY: I don't know what (1) _we're going to do_ (we / do). We've hardly made any money for ages.

NIGEL: I think we should advertise. We can send out leaflets.

MARY: Yes. (2) _That'll probably get_ (That / probably / get) the shop more widely known. But do you think (3) .... (people / come) here?

NIGEL: Well, we could try to get more online sales.

MARY: Yes, we need to improve our website. (4) .... (I / phone) the designer. And what about advertising on local radio?

NIGEL: Good idea. (5) .... (I / phone) them?

MARY: OK, thanks.

Tuesday

MARY: We haven't got enough money to pay for radio advertising and updating the website. I've been in touch with the bank. (6) .... (I / see) a business advisor called William there on Friday.

NIGEL: (7) .... (he / help) us to get a loan, do you think?

MARY: I hope so.

Friday

WILLIAM: So you want to borrow some money. How do you want to spend it?

MARY: (8) .... (We / advertise) on the radio and update our website. We've planned it carefully. We only need £5,000.

WILLIAM: OK. (9) .... (The bank / lend) you the money. But you must pay us back in three months. Can you do that?

MARY: (10) .... (We / do) it, I promise.

WILLIAM: Now, I just need a few more details, then (11) .... (I / help) you fill in the necessary forms.

MARY: Thank you.

WILLIAM: You're welcome.

The future: present continuous, will/shall, going to

Units 19–23

62

Complete the conversations. Use will/shall, going to or the present continuous.

A ANN: It just said on the radio that (1) _it's going to snow_ .
BILL: Oh, did it? I (2) _'ll take_ my big coat then.
JOE: Good idea. So (3) .... Come on, Bill. Let's go.

B ED: Jenny's had her baby.
GAIL: Really? That's wonderful! (4) .... her some flowers.
ED: (5) .... her this afternoon at the hospital.
(6) .... them to her for you if you want.
GAIL: (7) .... you? Thanks very much. In that case,
(8) .... and buy them right away.

C KEN: I haven't got a clean shirt. (9) .... one for me?
LILY: No, (10) .... You can do your own washing!

63

Write what you would say in these situations. Use will/shall, going to or the present continuous.

1 You make your friend a cup of sweet coffee, then she tells you she doesn't take sugar. Offer to make her another one.
You: _I'm sorry, I'll make you another one_

2 A colleague asks why you're leaving work early. Explain that you have arranged to meet your grandmother at the airport.
You: ....

3 Your brother lent you some money last week. Promise to pay him back at the weekend.
You: ....

4 Your sister has bought some clothes from a cheap website. You want to buy some too and you've asked her several times for the address, but she refuses to tell you. Ask why she refuses to tell you.
You: .... ?

5 You failed an exam last year. Since then you've been working hard. Tell your teacher it's because you're determined not to fail again.
You: ....

6 Your neighbour is playing loud music late at night. You get angry and ask him to turn the volume down.
You: .... ?

7 You've been offered a role in a film and have accepted. Tell your friends about it.
You: .... !

8 A friend is telling you about a travel scholarship she has won. Ask her which countries she plans to visit.
You: ....

English Grammar in Use Supplementary Exercises

The future: all forms

Units 19–25

64 Put the verbs into the correct form: present simple, present continuous, the **will/shall** future, the **going to** future, the future continuous or the future perfect.

A Mick is watching television when his sister Vanessa comes into the room.

MICK: What are you doing in your dressing-gown? It's only eight o'clock.

VANESSA: I don't feel well. (1) _I'm going to have_ (I / have) an early night.

MICK: Bad luck. I hope (2) _you feel_ (you / feel) better in the morning.

VANESSA: So do I. (3) _____ (I / meet) my new boss at ten o'clock.

MICK: I think (4) _____ (I / make) some tea when this programme (5) _____ (finish). (6) _____ (I / bring) you a cup?

VANESSA: No, don't bother. (7) _____ (I / try) and go straight to sleep. Thanks anyway.

MICK: OK. Sleep well.

B Sandy and Alison are students who have been sharing a flat. Sandy is leaving to do a course in the USA.

SANDY: It's hard saying goodbye after so long.

ALISON: Yeah. Remember to send me your phone number when (8) _____ (you / get) your new phone in the States. And you've promised to Skype® me.

SANDY: Yeah, we can do that a lot. But (9) _____ (I / probably / not / have) time the first few days because (10) _____ (my course / start) as soon as (11) _____ (I / arrive), and (12) _____ (I / spend) the weekend with some friends of my father's.

ALISON: I know, of course.

SANDY: Anyway, do you know what (13) _____ (you / do) this time the Sunday after next?

ALISON: (14) _____ (I / get) ready to go to London.

SANDY: OK. So, (15) _____ (I / Skype) you about three o'clock that Sunday afternoon.

ALISON: Great.

Can, could and be able to

Units 26–27

65 Choose the correct alternative.

1 Why did you walk from the station? You ~~could phone~~ / could have phoned me for a lift.
2 I loved staying with my grandparents when I was a child. They let me read all their books and told me I could go / was able to go to bed as late as I wanted.
3 This carpet was priced at £500, but I could get / was able to get a discount because of this little mark in the corner.
4 I couldn't have found / haven't been able to find my mobile for days. It's making my life impossible!
5 I've no idea where my brother is now. He can be / could be at the North Pole for all I know.
6 It's hard to imagine how scientists cope with the Antarctic climate. I'm sure I can't / couldn't.
7 We could cook / could have cooked in our holiday flat, but we preferred to eat out.

66 Tick (✓) the best sentence in each pair, or tick both if both are possible.

1 a I broke my new necklace but luckily my sister could fix it for me. ✗
  b I broke my new necklace but luckily my sister was able to fix it for me. ✓

2 a Emily was with Tom when her phone was stolen, so she could use his to call me.
  b Emily was with Tom when her phone was stolen, so she was able to use his to call me.

3 a I didn't enjoy the match because I forgot my glasses. I couldn't see the ball.
  b I didn't enjoy the match because I forgot my glasses. I wasn't able to see the ball.

4 a In the end, Marion could come with us because her meeting was cancelled.
  b In the end, Marion was able to come with us because her meeting was cancelled.

5 a Bob couldn't speak Dutch when he arrived in Holland, but he's almost fluent now.
  b Bob wasn't able to speak Dutch when he arrived in Holland, but he's almost fluent now.

6 a I'd planned to get a taxi after the party, but luckily I could have a lift with Kate.
  b I'd planned to get a taxi after the party, but luckily I was able to have a lift with Kate.

7 a We really wanted to buy a new car last year, but we just couldn't afford it.
  b We really wanted to buy a new car last year, but we just weren't able to afford it.

8 a My brother could read well by the age of seven, but he had problems with maths.
  b My brother was able to read well by the age of seven, but he had problems with maths.

9 a Last night we heard a noise outside our window and when we turned off the light inside, we could see a fox by the rubbish bin.
  b Last night we heard a noise outside our window and when we turned off the light inside, we were able to see a fox by the rubbish bin.

10 a One day last week I locked my sister out of the house by mistake, but luckily she could get in through an open window!
   b One day last week I locked my sister out of the house by mistake, but luckily she was able to get in through an open window!

May and might

Units 29–30

67 Answer the questions with **might** or **might have** and the ideas in brackets.

1 What flavour ice cream shall we buy for Liz, vanilla or strawberry?
   (prefer chocolate) _She might prefer chocolate._

2 Why is Alan in such a bad mood today?
   (sleep badly last night) _He might have slept badly last night._

3 Why didn't Jane come to the party with her boyfriend last night?
   (have a row) _____

4 Why is Anna looking under the desk?
   (drop something) _____

5 I can't remember where I put my bag. Do you?
   (be under the bed) _____

6 Why hasn't anybody said 'Happy Birthday' to me?
   (plan a surprise) _____

7 Why does Henry look so miserable?
   (have some bad news) _____

8 Why isn't Sophie in the office today?
   (work at home) _____

9 Why didn't Rosemary come to the cinema last night?
   (have something better to do) _____

68 Use **might** to complete the sentences which explain why you should follow this advice.

1 You should reserve a seat on the train for long journeys.
   If you don't, _you might have to stand all the way_.

2 You'd better not leave your laptop in the garden.
   If you do, _someone might steal it_.

3 You should use a SatNav when you drive in London.
   If you don't, _____.

4 You should allow plenty of time to go through security checks at the airport.
   If you don't, _____.

5 You ought not to eat too much fast food.
   If you do, _____.

6 You'd better revise thoroughly before your exam.
   If you don't, _____.

7 You should have your car serviced regularly.
   If you don't, _____.

8 You shouldn't go clubbing the night before you start a new job.
   If you do, _____.

9 You ought to arrive punctually for meetings with your boss.
   If you don't, _____.

10 You shouldn't shout at your brother.
   If you do, _____.

English Grammar in Use Supplementary Exercises

Can, could, may, might, must and can't

Units 26–30

69 Match the beginning of each sentence with the most suitable ending.

1 You must have met some fascinating people	a after all your hard work.	1 _d_
2 You must know Tokyo is expensive	b after touring the world for years.	2 ....
3 You can't have lived in Tunisia for ten years	c if you've lived there.	3 ....
4 You can't be tired	~~d during your trip to Africa.~~	4 ....
5 You must be exhausted	e when you've just had a holiday.	5 ....
6 You may find it difficult to settle down	f without learning some Arabic.	6 ....
7 You couldn't have gone on holiday	g to the airport tomorrow.	7 ....
8 You might think about going to Spain	h because you had no money.	8 ....
9 You could take a taxi	i for your next holiday.	9 ....

70 Complete the email with the words from the box.

> may be seeing   may not have done   could have fallen
> ~~may have left~~   couldn't have left   may be visiting
> could be coming   may have found

From: Robin Nicholas
To: Helena Shakespeare
Subject: Seeing you again

Hi Helena,

It was good to see you last week and show you our research facilities here. Thanks for your email. Sorry to hear you lost your iPod on the journey home. I've looked for it, but it definitely isn't in our office. I think you (1) _may have left_ it on the train. Why not phone the lost property office? It (2) .... down the side of your seat. Someone (3) .... it and handed it in. Of course, if they like music, they (4) .... ! Anyway, as far as I remember, you (5) .... it here, because you were listening to it on the way to the station.

And now my news. Guess what? I (6) .... to your part of the world next month for a conference! My professor wanted to attend it, but now he's heard that some important scientists (7) .... our laboratory at that time. So, you and I (8) .... each other sooner than we expected. I'll email as soon as I know for certain.

All the best,
Robin

Can, could, may, might, must and can't — Units 26–30

71 Choose the correct alternative.

1 You <u>must be</u> / ~~can't be~~ very proud of your daughter winning the race.
2 I expected my boyfriend to call after work last night, but he didn't. I suppose he <u>must be</u> / <u>must have been</u> too tired.
3 That group is so famous now, it <u>must be / can't be</u> easy to get tickets to see them perform.
4 I'm sure we can get online here if we try. We <u>must be using / can't be using</u> the right password.
5 I've just rung the garage to check whether they've fixed my car, but I can't get an answer. I suppose they <u>may have / may be having</u> a break in the yard.
6 I don't know why you wanted to stay at that party. You <u>might have enjoyed / can't have enjoyed</u> talking to all those boring people.
7 I can't go out this morning. We're getting a new TV and the store <u>may be delivering / must be delivering</u> it today.
8 Please check these figures again. They're not accurate. You <u>might have been concentrating / can't have been concentrating</u> when you added them up.
9 You <u>must be / must have been</u> thirsty after playing tennis all afternoon. Shall I get you a drink?

72 Complete the answers with **must**, **can't** or **might** and any other words you need.

1 GERALD: Can that be James phoning at this hour? It's gone midnight!
  HILDA: It _might be_ him. He said he'd phone if he passed his exam.

2 JIM: There's a light on in that office block. Do you think it's a thief?
  HARRY: It _must be_ the cleaners. They always work at night.

3 WILL: What are we having for Sunday dinner?
  TESSA: It _____ chicken. Mum often does chicken on Sundays.

4 CLARE: Is that your daughter's coat?
  FIONA: No, it _____ hers. It's much too big.

5 ANDY: Where did I put my trainers? I can't remember.
  JANE: They _____ the car. You often leave them there.

6 ELINOR: Where did Adam get that new guitar? He hasn't got any money.
  KATE: It _____ a present. After all, it was his birthday last week.

7 NICKY: Why did Mina ignore me at the party last night?
  RYAN: She _____ you. She wasn't wearing her glasses.

8 EMMA: Do you think Cindy told the boss I left work early yesterday?
  NEIL: She's away this week, so she _____ him.

9 JILL: What's making me feel so ill?
  PAT: It _____ ate. Did you have seafood last night? That sometimes makes people ill.

Must(n't), need(n't), should(n't) and don't have to

Units 31–33

73 Match the beginning of each sentence with the most suitable ending.

1 Lucy should be having breakfast,
2 Patsy shouldn't go clubbing all night
3 Jenny shouldn't have gone out
4 Megan mustn't oversleep
5 Nicky doesn't have to get up yet
6 Natalie didn't need to hurry
7 Sharon needn't have set the alarm clock

a when she was supposed to be studying.
b because she woke up early anyway.
c ~~but she's too nervous to eat.~~
d when she has an exam the next day.
e if she's not going to work today.
f or she'll be late for her interview.
g because she wasn't late.

1 .....c.....
2 ....
3 ....
4 ....
5 ....
6 ....
7 ....

74 Choose the correct alternative.

Thursday

NEIL: We're doing our presentation to the seminar group next Monday. Can you email them right away?
ROBBIE: (1) Must I do / ~~Should I do~~ it now?
NEIL: Well, we (2) must have told / should have told them earlier really.
ROBBIE: Oh, all right then.

Friday

NAOMI: I've had an email about Neil and Robbie's presentation on Monday.
ELLIE: That's strange, I haven't. Do you think I (3) must / ought to call them?
NAOMI: No, you (4) mustn't / don't have to. It's probably not relevant to your research area.

Monday

NAOMI: Hi, Neil. I've come a bit early in case you wanted help to get the room ready. But I see I (5) needn't bother / needn't have bothered, you've got everything organised!
NEIL: Isn't Ellie with you?
NAOMI: No, she didn't get an email from you, so we thought the presentation wasn't relevant to her work.
NEIL: Oh, dear. Robbie (6) must send / must have sent the email to the wrong address.
NAOMI: Where he is now? He (7) must be / should be here.
NEIL: I don't know. He (8) must have forgotten / should have forgotten we're doing this presentation. He's so unreliable!

Must(n't), need(n't), should(n't) and don't have to

Units 31–33

75
For each pair of sentences, write *same* if sentences *a* and *b* have the same meaning. If the meaning is different, try to explain.

1. a It is vital to wear a helmet when you ride a motorbike.
   b You must wear a helmet when you ride a motorbike.   *same*

2. a I expect we'll get the contract because we offered the best price.
   b We offered the best price, so we should get the contract.   ....

3. a It isn't necessary for us to spend a long time in the museum if it's not interesting.
   b We shouldn't spend a long time in the museum if it's not interesting.   ....

4. a It was wrong of you to open the package.
   b You must have opened the package.   ....

5. a She promised to phone me before lunch. It's seven o'clock now.
   b She should have phoned me by now.   ....

6. a I made far more sandwiches than we needed.
   b I needn't make so many sandwiches.   ....

7. a It's essential that my father doesn't find out what I've done.
   b My father must have found out what I've done.   ....

8. a In my opinion it would be wrong for them to move house now.
   b I don't think they need to move house now.   ....

9. a My sister offered me a lift, so it wasn't necessary for me to call a taxi.
   b As my sister offered me a lift, I didn't need to call a taxi.   ....

10. a I think it's a good idea to check the timetable before we leave.
    b We should have checked the timetable before we left.   ....

76
Complete the sentences with must(n't), needn't or should(n't).

1. My phone's out of credit. I ....*must*........ top it up before I do anything else.
2. You .... finish that essay tonight if you're too tired. Midday tomorrow is the deadline.
3. What are you doing here? .... you be at college?
4. He really .... have told his brother about this present. It was supposed to be a secret.
5. You .... pay to go into this exhibition because I've got my membership card with me.
6. You .... make so much noise. We'll be asked to leave the restaurant if you don't stop shouting.
7. I'm going to be in trouble. I .... have texted my mum earlier this afternoon and I completely forgot.
8. You .... have gone to the bus station, you can book tickets online.

English Grammar in Use Supplementary Exercises

Must(n't), need(n't), should(n't) and don't have to

Units 31–33

77 Read the rules of the Fitness Centre. Complete what the instructor says with **must(n't)**, **need(n't)** or **should(n't)**.

SPORTS CLUB NOTICE

- It is vital to have a health check before using the gym for the first time.
- It isn't necessary for members to pay for towels, but guests are charged £1 per towel.
- It is recommended that you begin with light exercises to warm up.
- It is not recommended that you exercise after a heavy meal.
- It's a good idea to ask a member of staff if you're not sure how to use the equipment.
- It is forbidden to use the Fitness Centre against the advice of the staff.

You (1) _must_ have a health check before using the gym for the first time.
You (2) .... pay for towels, but your guests (3) .... pay £1.
You (4) .... begin with light exercises to warm up.
You (5) .... exercise after a heavy meal.
You (6) .... ask a member of staff if you're not sure how to use the equipment.
You (7) .... use the Fitness Centre against the advice of the staff.

78 Read what James did. Then complete what the instructor says with **must(n't)**, **need(n't)** or **should(n't)**.

James became a member of the Sports Club yesterday. He used the gym without having a health check. He paid for a towel. He didn't begin with light exercises. He exercised soon after eating a big lunch. He didn't ask a member of staff how to use the equipment. His back is very painful today.

James (1) .... have used the gym without having a health check, so it's not my fault his back is very painful.
He (2) .... have paid for a towel.
He (3) .... have begun with light exercises.
He (4) .... have exercised soon after lunch.
He (5) .... have asked me how to use the equipment.
He (6) .... have injured his back.

(Don't) have to, should(n't), had better (not) and ought (not) to

Units 31, 33, 35

79

Read the situations and write sentences with **ought (not) to**. Some of the sentences are past and some are present.

1 Andy is very shy. His teacher chose him to make a speech to the whole school.
   His teacher _ought not to have chosen Andy to make a speech to the whole school_.

2 Carla has an exam on Monday. She plans to spend the weekend at a music festival.
   She _____.

3 I live in Kyoto. You went there last week, but you didn't visit me.
   You _____.

4 Dan has a new MP3 player. His children used it without his permission.
   They _____.

5 You've bought a new phone. The shop said it had unlimited texts, but it has only ten a day.
   They _____.

6 We wanted to fly home at the weekend, but the flights were all full. We hadn't booked seats.
   We _____.

80

Tick (✓) the correct sentence in each pair, or tick both if both are correct.

1 *a* You should always lock your front door when you go out. ✓
   b You'd better always lock your front door when you go out.

2 *a* I should leave now or I'll miss my bus.
   b I'd better leave now or I'll miss my bus.

3 *a* I don't think people should keep pets if they don't have time to care for them properly.
   b I don't think people had better keep pets if they don't have time to care for them properly.

4 *a* If you want to take photos here, you should ask permission or we might get into trouble.
   b If you want to take photos here, you'd better ask permission or we might get into trouble.

5 *a* You should wear a coat. It's cold outside.
   b You'd better wear a coat. It's cold outside.

6 *a* Would you mind getting stamps when you're out? The money I gave you should be enough.
   b Would you mind getting stamps when you're out? The money I gave you had better be enough.

7 *a* I realise you must be surprised to see us. Perhaps I should explain what's going on.
   b I realise you must be surprised to see us. Perhaps I'd better explain what's going on.

8 *a* People really should wear a helmet when they ride a bike.
   b People really had better wear a helmet when they ride a bike.

9 *a* Passengers on long flights should move their legs as much as possible.
   b Passengers on long flights had better move their legs as much as possible.

10 *a* Tell Jess that she should bring some cash if we're going out tonight.
   b Tell Jess that she'd better bring some cash if we're going out tonight.

(Don't) have to, should(n't), had better (not) and ought (not) to

Units 31, 33, 35

81
Complete the email with **had better**, **should** or **have to**. Sometimes there is more than one answer.

> **From:** Anna James.com
> **To:** Gary Newlands
> **Subject:** Travel tips
>
> Gary,
> I know you haven't done such a long flight before so I thought I (1) _'d better_ give you a few tips. First, you (2) .... make sure you get to the airport really early because you always (3) .... spend ages getting through security. You (4) .... be prepared for them to open all your hand luggage too. Your flight is an early one so, with luck, you (5) .... be able to get a seat in the business lounge. You (6) .... (not) pay for breakfast as it's free there. When your flight's called, you (7) .... start moving to the gate immediately because sometimes you (8) .... walk for about fifteen minutes. You (9) .... (not) take very heavy hand luggage because you (10) .... carry it yourself and you can't take a trolley to the gates. Everyone agrees there (11) .... be some, of course, but there aren't. You get a meal on the flight of course, and you (12) .... eat it even if it doesn't taste very interesting, because there's nowhere to eat until you reach your hotel at the other end. If you have any questions, email me.
> Regards, Anna

82
Complete the second sentence with **(don't) have to**, **should (not)** or **had better (not)** so that it has a similar meaning to the first.

1 It is compulsory to wear a helmet when you ride a motorbike.
You _have to wear a helmet when you ride a motorbike_.

2 It's advisable to check that all the windows are shut whenever you go out.
You ....

3 It's not acceptable to borrow money from people you hardly know.
You ....

4 I suggest we keep the door shut in case someone sees us.
You ....

5 Training regularly is essential if you want to succeed in athletics.
You ....

6 I don't think it's a good idea to take your phone to the beach. It might get stolen.
You ....

7 It'd be a good idea to change your shirt before the guests arrive.
You ....

8 There is no extra charge for delivery.
You ....

Should

83 Tick (✓) the correct sentences.

1. a After a match, the captain insists the football team should take things easy. ✓
   b After a match, the captain insists the football team take things easy. ✓
   c After a match, the captain insists the football team to take things easy.

2. a The journalist demanded that the minister resigned.
   b The journalist demanded that the minister resign.
   c The journalist demanded that the minister should resign.

3. a If you really want to get rich fast, I suggest you should work harder.
   b If you really want to get rich fast, I suggest you work harder.
   c If you really want to get rich fast, I suggest you to work harder.

4. a He never has any money, so it's very odd that he have a new car.
   b He never has any money, so it's very odd that he has a new car.
   c He never has any money, so it's very odd that he should have a new car.

5. a I think the weather will stay dry, but you can borrow my raincoat if by any chance it rains.
   b I think the weather will stay dry, but you can borrow my raincoat if by any chance it should rain.
   c I think the weather will stay dry, but you can borrow my raincoat if by any chance it rained.

6. a My doctor explained that it was important I should take more exercise.
   b My doctor explained that it was important I take more exercise.
   c My doctor explained that it was important I took more exercise.

84 There are mistakes in five of these sentences. Correct the sentences where necessary. Write 'OK' if the sentence is already correct.

1. We were very surprised <u>that Tom behave in such</u> a rude manner. — *that Tom behaved / that Tom should behave*

2. I asked a friend about getting train tickets and he recommended to book online.

3. The government accepted the recommendation that they reduce spending on the armed services.

4. If I can't use a phone here, how do you suggest me to contact my offce?

5. I shouldn't go in there if I were you. They're having an argument about money.

6. Should be my phone off when you call, just leave a message on voicemail.

7. It's essential that I should see the doctor today.

8. Why didn't you demand the club to refund your subscription?

Should

Units 33–34

85 Complete the conversation with **should** where necessary. Leave out **should** where possible.

BEN: We've got a review of the company's environmental footprint today and I can't find our latest energy consumption figures. What (1) _should I do_ (I / do)?

SUE: I really don't know. It's odd that (2) _the figures disappear_ (the figures / disappear) just when you need them. Did you ask Rose?

BEN: Yes. She insisted that (3) _I check_ (I / check) all the files myself.

SUE: She's so unhelpful.

BEN: And where's Jack? He promised to update me on new machinery costs.

SUE: I saw him printing off some figures a few minutes ago.

BEN: It's important (4) _we discuss_ (we / discuss) his report before the meeting.

SUE: Shall I go and find him?

BEN: No, (5) _I shouldn't bother_ (I / not / bother). He's probably on his way.

SUE: OK. Are you going to stay in the office over lunchtime?

BEN: Yes. It's vital (6) _I find_ (I / find) these figures for this afternoon's meeting.

SUE: Oh, right. Well, I'm going out to give a talk to some new graduates about our industry this afternoon, so, if (7) _anyone calls_ (anyone / call), will you say I'm not available till tomorrow?

BEN: Are we going to recruit new staff?

SUE: Well, I'd like to, but the accountant's recommendation is that (8) _we wait_ (we / wait) until later in the year. He says we can't afford anyone yet. He suggests (9) _we hire_ (we / hire) someone temporary if we really have to.

BEN: I suppose it's only natural (10) _he should be_ (he / be) cautious. But we could really do with permanent help.

SUE: Yes, quite.

Modals: review

Units 26–35

86 Use your own ideas to complete the sentences.

1. In most countries motorcyclists must _wear a helmet_.
2. I nearly missed the first class this morning. I should have ....
3. I decided I didn't like the shoes I'd bought, but luckily I was able to ....
4. The shops are always terribly crowded on Saturdays, so I may ....
5. Politicians ought not to ....
6. Some people dislike flying, so they might ....
7. Most people pass the driving test first time, so it can't ....
8. I don't know why my brother hasn't phoned. He may have ....
9. If you really want to get fit, you should ....
10. When the price of petrol rose sharply, many people had to ....
11. Can you imagine travelling before the invention of railways? It must have ....
12. Commuter trains are often overcrowded, and people aren't able to ....
13. I could .... when I was ten, but I couldn't ....
14. That girl looks as if she's lost. We'd better ....

87 Read this notice. Then complete the advice for people who are coming to your school or place of work.

Information for newcomers to London Language Institute

- You shouldn't miss lessons.
- You should bring your laptop if you have one.
- You mustn't be late for class.
- You must switch your phone off during lessons.
- You needn't bring a dictionary.
- You don't have to take any exams.

Information for newcomers to ....

1. You shouldn't ....
2. You should ....
3. You mustn't ....
4. You must ....
5. You needn't ....
6. You don't have to ....

If I do and If I did

Units 25, 38–39

88

Choose the correct alternative.

1 If <u>I miss</u> / <s>I'll miss</s> lunch, I'll get a sandwich later.
2 We'll have to leave without John if <u>he doesn't arrive</u> / <u>he won't arrive</u> soon.
3 They <u>won't refund</u> / <u>didn't refund</u> your money if you haven't kept your receipt.
4 Will you send me a text when <u>you reach</u> / <u>you'll reach</u> Mexico City?
5 If I make some coffee, <u>do you cut</u> / <u>will you cut</u> the cake?
6 <u>Did you work</u> / <u>Would you work</u> harder if you were better paid?
7 If you <u>don't complain</u> / <u>didn't complain</u> so much, you might be more popular.
8 <u>Weren't my friends</u> / <u>Wouldn't my friends be</u> envious if they could only see me now!

89

Complete the sentences using words and phrases from the box.

| would it help | <s>will she say</s> | will you do |
| will it cost | would you buy | would you say |

1 EVA: I don't know what's happened to the bag I borrowed from Jo.
　SUE: What *will she say* if you don't find it?
　EVA: I suppose she'll be very annoyed.

2 TIM: I'm thinking of applying to do my MSc abroad.
　ANN: Really? What .... if you do that?
　TIM: About 10,000 Euros, I think.

3 MAY: I don't know how I'm going to pay my rent this week.
　LEE: So, ... if I lent you some money?
　MAY: Well, yes, of course. But I can't borrow from you.
　LEE: Don't be silly. How much do you want?

4 PAUL: I wish I could afford a new car.
　TINA: What .... if you could afford one?
　PAUL: Oh, I wouldn't mind what it was – as long as it didn't keep breaking down.

5 BILL: I don't think I'm going to pass my driving test next week.
　BEN: What .... if you don't?
　BILL: I'll have to take it again. I need it to get the job I want.

6 JO: Where's my bag? You know, the one I lent to you.
　EVA: Oh. What .... if I'd lost it?
　JO: I'd tell you to get me a new one!

If I do and If I did

Units 25, 38–39

90 Put the verbs into the correct form.

1 If I had more money, ...would you marry... (you / marry) me?
2 The teacher wouldn't help you if .... (he / not / like) you.
3 .... (you / see) what the hotel looks like if you look at the website.
4 .... (your boyfriend / not / be) amazed if he could see you now?
5 If .... (I / not / revise) thoroughly, I may not get a good mark.
6 If you wanted to buy your dad a present, what .... (you / look for)?
7 Sally would have a lot more friends if .... (she / not / be) so mean.
8 How .... (you / feel) if you were in my situation?
9 Would you change your job if .... (you / can)?

91 Lisa and Trish are students. They're talking about what to do after university. Write sentences using the words given.

TRISH: Do you have any plans for next year?
LISA: Well, I don't have much money. But I speak Portuguese and Spanish. So (1) I / travel / if I / afford it.
   I'd travel if I could afford it.
TRISH: (2) If you / find / a job using your languages / you / take it?

LISA: (3) If it / be / in South America / I / certainly / consider it carefully.

I've always wanted to go there.
TRISH: What about working as a tour guide, taking tourists round?
(4) That / be / a great way to travel if you / speak the right languages.

LISA: But (5) I / only / consider / a job like that if I / be / sure the travel company was a good one.

(6) If the tourists / not / like / their hotels and so on, I / have a terrible time.

TRISH: Yes. (7) You / be / handling complaints every day if they / not / be / happy.

LISA: Exactly! (8) But if I / decide / to apply for a job like that, / you / help me with my application?

TRISH: Of course. And, I'm sure (9) you / succeed, if you / do.

LISA: Thanks very much.

54   English Grammar in Use Supplementary Exercises

If I do and If I did

Units 25, 38–39

92 Write questions using if for the following answers.

1. *What would you do if someone gave you a diamond necklace?* — I'd probably give it to my mother.
2. _____? — I'd share it with my friends.
3. _____? — I'd call the police.
4. _____? — We'd get out as fast as we could.
5. _____? — I'd ask my teacher's advice about it.
6. _____? — He'd be extremely angry.
7. _____? — She'd probably fall over.
8. _____? — I'd be late for work.
9. _____? — We'd sail around the world.
10. _____? — They'd never make any money.
11. _____? — There'd be no more wars.
12. _____? — I'd stay at home all day.

93 Look at the questions you wrote for Exercise 92. Now write new answers of your own to your questions.

1. What would you do if someone gave you a diamond necklace?
   I'd sell it and buy a horse.
2. _____
3. _____
4. _____
5. _____
6. _____
7. _____
8. _____
9. _____
10. _____
11. _____
12. _____

If I did and If I had done

Units 39–40

94
Match the beginning of each sentence with the most suitable ending.

1 If you had been promoted,
2 If you were rude to the boss,
3 If you were promoted,
4 If you hadn't been promoted,
5 If you had lost your job,
6 If you apologised,
7 If you were fired,

a you'd be able to change the system.
b would you have left the firm?
c you wouldn't be sacked.
d you wouldn't get a reference.
e ~~would you have made any changes?~~
f you'd probably regret it later.
g you'd have been very upset.

1 _e_
2 ......
3 ......
4 ......
5 ......
6 ......
7 ......

95
Complete the conversations with suitable verbs.

1 SEAN: Why didn't you go to the lecture last night?
   JIM: I didn't know about it.
   SEAN: So _would you have gone_ if you _had known_ ?

2 JILL: Jane's got a PhD, hasn't she?
   MILLY: Yeah. I don't know why she works in this lab. I .... something worthwhile if I .... her qualifications.
   JILL: What kind of work would you do?
   MILLY: Oh, I don't know exactly. But if I .... Jane, I .... to do original research.

3 SAM: Why did you ask Veronica about her boyfriend? It really upset her.
   MICK: Well, I didn't realise they'd split up.
   SAM: You didn't know, then?
   MICK: Of course not. If I .... , I .... her about him.

4 TIM: Hey, I've got a text from Cheryl!
   PAT: Look out! Mind the step.
   TIM: Ouch! I've hurt my knee.
   PAT: Well, you .... it if you .... that text.

5 JOHN: Do you love me?
   ROSE: You know I do.
   JOHN: Would you .... me if I .... poor?
   ROSE: Probably. But fortunately you're rich.
   JOHN: Well, yes, I am. But if I .... all my money, what .... ?
   ROSE: I'd say goodbye.
   JOHN: Now you're joking.
   ROSE: Oh no, I'm not!

English Grammar in Use Supplementary Exercises

If I did and If I had done

Units 39–40

96

Read the article. For each number, write a comment beginning with **If**.

Singing star Tanya announces wedding plans
— exclusive interview with Charlie Green

CHARLIE: Well, congratulations Tanya.
TANYA: Thank you. Of course, we're very excited about getting married, and frantically busy too, needless to say.
CHARLIE: I'm sure all your fans are longing to know how you met your fiance, Dr Radani.
TANYA: Well, it's a funny story really. (1) You know I did a world tour last year? That meant I had to spend five months travelling. (2) And I didn't have a holiday last year so I got terribly tired and stressed. (3) My manager panicked because he had contracted me to record a new album after the tour. (4) Anyway, the tour was such a huge success that I was able to postpone the recording for two months. I was really relieved. (5) My manager sent me to a luxury spa hotel for a complete rest. And I met this wonderful man, Hossein. He's a scientist. (6) He told me he should have been doing research in California, but he was recovering from a bad skiing accident. (7) We were the only guests on our own, so we started talking. (8) He didn't know who I was. He didn't treat me like a star. He made me laugh. It was such a change. And that was it really. We found we'd fallen in love. (9) Wasn't it lucky my manager panicked? That's how I met my fiance!
CHARLIE: And what about your wedding plans?
TANYA: Ah, they're completely secret.

1 If she hadn't done a world tour last year, she wouldn't have spent five months travelling.

2

3

4

5

6

7

8

9

English Grammar in Use Supplementary Exercises

If I did and If I had done

Units 39–40

97
What would you say in each situation? Begin each sentence with If.

1. yesterday / today
If I hadn't dyed my hair, my friends wouldn't be laughing at me.

2. yesterday / today
If I hadn't revised thoroughly, I wouldn't be able to do the test.

3. yesterday / today

4. this morning / now
"I haven't got time for breakfast!"
"I can't concentrate."

5. last week / now
"I must remember to phone and book seats."

6. 8 am / 9.30 am
"Oh damn!"
"You're fired!"

7. last weekend / today
"I'm sorry I won't be at the wedding."

8. this afternoon / now
"Do we need to stop for petrol?"
"No, we've got more than enough to get home."

Conditionals: review

Units 25, 38–40

98 Use your own ideas to complete the sentences.

1 What will you do if *your plane is delayed* ?
2 If he .... he'd have more friends.
3 If I hadn't mended the TV, we ....
4 You wouldn't have felt ill if you ....
5 She .... if she didn't gossip about her friends.
6 Will you forgive me if I .... ?
7 If I .... what would happen?
8 She would have won the competition if she ....
9 They wouldn't have minded if we ....
10 He .... if he had listened to my advice.

99 For each pair of sentences, complete sentence b so that it means the same as sentence a.

1 a You should go swimming regularly because that's a good way to get fit.
  b If you *go swimming regularly, you'll get* fit.
2 a Flying to Scotland is cheaper than going by rail. As a result, people go there by plane.
  b If flying *weren't (wasn't) cheaper* than going by rail, people *wouldn't go* there by plane.
3 a Cutting down rainforests has caused many plants and animals to disappear.
  b Many plants and animals *wouldn't have disappeared* if people *hadn't cut down* rainforests.
4 a I can't take a lot of exercise because I don't have enough free time.
  b If I .... more free time, I ....
5 a Many students leave their bikes unlocked in the college yard. This makes life easy for thieves.
  b If students .... in the college yard, life ....
6 a Some people didn't realise how dangerous smoking was when they were young. Now they are older they have serious health problems.
  b If people .... when they were young, they .... now they are older.
7 a Petra made some bread, but it didn't rise because she forgot to add yeast.
  b The bread .... if Petra ....
8 a It's important to protect wildlife now. Otherwise there will be nothing left for future generations.
  b If we .... , there .... for future generations.
9 a Children don't realise how much toys cost, so they don't understand why they can't always have new ones.
  b If children .... , they .... why they can't always have new ones.

I wish

Units 39–41

100 Look at the pictures and write what each person wishes, using the words given.

1. be / tall and strong
   I wish I were tall and strong.
   or I wish I was tall and strong.

2. have / car

3. work / office

4. live / with my son

5. can / swim

6. not / live / city

7. be / helicopter pilot

8. not / have / short hair

I wish

Units 39–41

101 Bernie and Martin share a room at college. Read what they say about each other.
Then write sentences beginning **I wish he would / wouldn't**.

MARTIN

It's dreadful having to share a room with Bernie. He borrows my phone without asking. He never washes his coffee mug and he's so untidy! He leaves his shoes lying around the room and drops his clothes on my chair – the room's such a mess I can't work. And he comes in late in the evening and doesn't remember I go to sleep early. Then he lies in bed playing computer games. I can't stand it! I'm going to look for a room on my own.

BERNIE

The trouble with Martin is that he never relaxes. He works so hard. He gets angry when I just make a phone call. And he interferes with my possessions. He moves my shoes and clothes around so I can't find them. He throws my shoes on my bed. He never plays computer games with me. He wakes me up when he goes out for a run early in the morning. He's no fun to share a room with.

Martin says:
I wish Bernie wouldn't borrow my phone without asking.
....
....
....

Bernie says:
I wish Martin would relax sometimes.
....
....
....

English Grammar in Use Supplementary Exercises

I wish

102 Complete the conversations using wish.

1 SUE: My mother's really angry with me.
PAM: Why?
SUE: Because she's found out where I was last weekend.
PAM: Oh, yes. I told her.
SUE: Well, I *wish you hadn't told* (not / tell) her. It's not your business.
PAM: I'm sorry.

2 TONY: Have you seen Ben's new jacket? I bet it was expensive.
ANA: He told me it cost him 700 Euros.
TONY: Wow! I _____ (have) as much money as him.
ANA: Well, you may not be rich, but you're much better looking than Ben.
TONY: Am I?

3 GARY: You seem to enjoy dancing with Luke.
JANE: Yes, I do. He's a very good dancer.
GARY: I _____ (learn) to dance when I was young.
JANE: You could learn now.
GARY: Oh, I'd feel stupid in a dancing class at my age.

4 EVA: I went to Indonesia last month.
MAY: Really? My brother's working in Jakarta now.
EVA: I _____ (realise). I could have met up with him.
MAY: Yes, it's a pity. You must tell me if you're going there again.

5 FRED: My parents moved to São Paolo last month.
ALI: How do they like it?
FRED: My mother likes it, but my father misses the sea. He _____ (not / move) there.
ALI: Perhaps he'll get used to it.
FRED: I doubt it.

6 LUCY: You haven't seen my MP3 player, have you?
CHLOE: No, I haven't.
LUCY: I _____ (know) what I'd done with it.
CHLOE: I hope you didn't leave it in the taxi last night.
LUCY: So do I!

7 KAY: My brothers are digging a swimming pool.
JILL: That sounds like hard work!
KAY: It is. Actually, I suspect they _____ (never / start). But they can't stop now. There's a great big hole in the middle of the garden!
JILL: Yes, I see what you mean.

The passive

Units 42–45

103 Complete the sentences using words from each box.

| build | design | develop | discover | discover |
| invent | invent | ~~name~~ | paint | play |

the Ancient Egyptians   Sir Tim Berners-Lee   the Chinese
Crick and Watson   Marie Curie   Gustave Eiffel   ~~Eric the Red~~
Johnny Depp   Guglielmo Marconi   Pablo Picasso

1 Greenland _was named by Eric the Red_ .
2 Captain Jack Sparrow ....
3 The Pyramids ....
4 The wireless ....
5 Guernica ....
6 The World Wide Web ....
7 The Statue of Liberty ....
8 The structure of DNA ....
9 Paper money ....
10 Radium ....

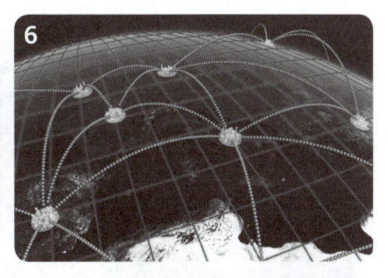

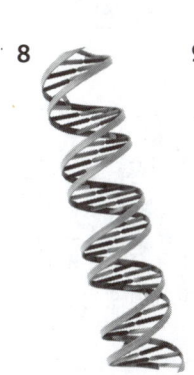

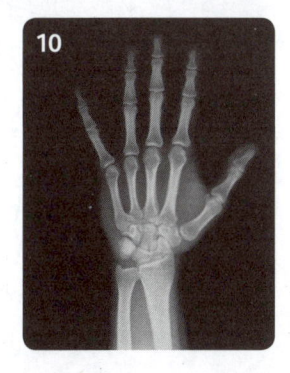

The passive   Units 42–45

104 Put the verbs into the correct present perfect form, active or passive (**has done** or **has been done**).

1. the woman / open
   The woman has opened it.

2. the fruit / eat
   The fruit has been eaten.

3. the puncture / mend

4. the concert / cancel

5. Jane Jones / elect

6. the rabbit / disappear

7. the sculpture / steal

8. the students / pass

The passive

Units 42–45

105
Rewrite this article using passive forms of the underlined verbs.

DARING RAID AT LOCAL HOTEL

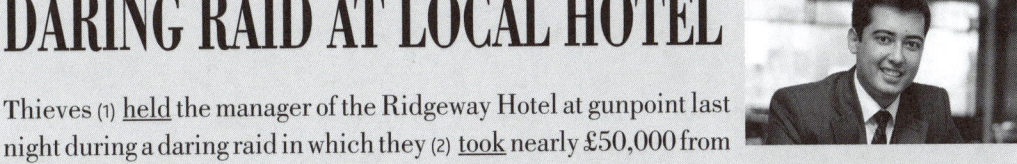

Thieves (1) held the manager of the Ridgeway Hotel at gunpoint last night during a daring raid in which they (2) took nearly £50,000 from the hotel safe. They also (3) broke into several of the bedrooms and (4) removed articles of value. The thieves made their escape through the kitchen, where they (5) damaged several pieces of equipment. They (6) injured the chef when he tried to stop them and (7) left him lying unconscious on the floor. Police (8) arrested the thieves early this morning.

1 The manager of the Ridgeway Hotel was held at gunpoint last night.
2
3
4
5
6
7
8

106
Put the verbs into the correct passive form.

1 I've collected all the documents that _are needed_ (need) for the house sale. Can you take them to the lawyer's office _to be signed_ (sign)?
2 Look, this is a secret. Come into the garden where we _____ (not / overhear).
3 If you hadn't been so late for work, you _____ (not / sack).
4 This office is very inefficient. The phone _____ (never / answer) promptly, no proper records _____ (keep), and, worst of all, no reports _____ (written) since I started work here.
5 I was so worried about my garden while I was in hospital, but I have very good neighbours. When I got home, I could see that the vegetables _____ (water) every day and the grass _____ (cut) regularly.
6 Can you come to the police station? The man who _____ (suspect) of stealing your wallet _____ (arrest) and _____ (question) at the moment. The police hope he _____ (identify), either by you or another witness.
7 We had hoped to see several famous paintings, but the gallery _____ (reorganised) at the time of our visit and most of the really valuable works _____ (move) for safe keeping.

English Grammar in Use Supplementary Exercises

The passive

Units 42–45

107 There are mistakes in eight of these sentences. Correct the sentences where necessary. Write 'OK' if the sentence is already correct.

1. My neighbour is proud of her grandson who born last week. — who was born last week.
2. I'm very fond of this old brooch because it was belonged to my grandmother.
3. My family live in Dubai, but I was educated in Switzerland.
4. I'm afraid I can't lend you my car. It's repairing this week.
5. The bridge was collapsed during the floods, but fortunately no-one was using it at the time.
6. If you don't watch the barbecue carefully, someone will get burn.
7. The word 'stupid' was in my report, but it wasn't referred to you.
8. I'm sorry I'm late. I got held up in the traffic again.
9. When did you realise that your bag had been disappeared?
10. Children under the age of sixteen do not allow in the jacuzzi.

108 Choose the correct alternative.

Hi Sally,

How are you? I'm having a great time in Namibia. Our group is small and (1) we were looked after / we're being looked after very well by our guide. (2) We've been shown / We were shown some amazing things already and (3) we've seen / we've been seen some fantastic landscapes.

Last weekend we went to a National Park. (4) We were driven / We were driving to a watering hole where an amazing range of animals (5) could be seeing / could be seen. We were told that the numbers (6) were risen / have risen since the National Park (7) founded / was founded.

(8) I'd been warned / I'd been warning that the accommodation there was quite basic, but it was fine. (9) We were given / We were giving a big tent each, and there are outdoor showers and so on, which (10) are kept / have kept very clean.

Our guide tells us lots of funny stories. He (11) was sent / sent to South Africa by his family to work in a bank, but he (12) hated / was hated it. So he (13) has behaved / behaved very badly in order to (14) get sacked / got sacked. He kept us laughing for hours.

Tomorrow (15) we'll be joined / we'll be joining another group and going to see some rock paintings. (16) They were discovered / They discovered quite recently, so we're one of the first groups (17) to be shown / to have shown them.

I'll email again when I can (18) get connected / have connected to the Internet.

Love,

Maurice

The passive

109

Complete the second sentence so that it has a similar meaning to the first sentence.
Do not use by unless it is important to the meaning.

1 The instructor has marked all the assignments.
   All the assignments have been marked .

2 My hairdresser kept me waiting for half an hour.
   I .

3 The students must pay their own fees for this course.
   The fees for this course .

4 Do you suppose your brother could have written that email?
   Do you suppose that email ?

5 Solar panels supply all the power for this house.
   All the power for this house .

6 During the summer, the cafe was employing more waiters every week.
   During the summer, more waiters .

7 Nobody informed the police that there had been a mistake.
   The police .

8 Where will your company send you next year?
   Where will you ?

9 The news about the war worried Josephine.
   Josephine .

10 I've still got the money because no-one has claimed it.
   I've still got the money because it .

11 Has anyone ever asked you for your opinion?
   Have you ?

12 People shouldn't allow children to watch that kind of TV programme.
   Children .

13 All visitors must wear identity badges.
   Identity badges .

14 Someone must have changed the time of the meeting.
   The time of the meeting .

15 When will someone deliver the food for the party?
   When ?

The passive Units 42–45

110 Put the verbs into the most suitable passive tense.

Alana has just met her boyfriend Grant in a coffee shop.

ALANA: Hi! Sorry I'm late.
GRANT: What kept you?
ALANA: I came on the bus and (1) *it was stuck* (it / stick) in a traffic jam for forty minutes.
GRANT: Why didn't you just walk across the park as usual?
ALANA: Because the park (2) .... (close) since last weekend.
GRANT: Why's that?
ALANA: A celebrity tennis tournament (3) .... (hold) there.
GRANT: Do you know who (4) .... (it / organise) by?
ALANA: No, but I think the Williams sisters are competing in it. Someone told me
(5) .... (they / see) at the Royal Hotel at the weekend.
GRANT: Really?
ALANA: Yeah. My friend said (6) .... (they / fly) here in a private plane by the organisers.
GRANT: Well, if it's true, we're not going to the disco at the Royal this Friday.
ALANA: Why not?
GRANT: If they're there, the hotel (7) .... (surround) by fans and security guards.
ALANA: But we might meet them if we go.
GRANT: Don't be silly. They won't go to our local disco. And
(8) .... (we / not invite) to their suite. In fact, the disco (9) .... (probably / cancel) if the hotel is full of celebrities.
ALANA: I suppose so. But we can go to the park gate now and see what's happening. I heard that some local people
(10) .... (recruit) yesterday, but I was too busy to go. Perhaps
(11) .... (we / employ) to sell programmes or something.
GRANT: OK, if you want to. But don't expect
(12) .... (allow) anywhere near the big stars.

68 English Grammar in Use Supplementary Exercises

The passive

Units 42–45

111 Complete the sentences with the correct form of **get** where possible and a form of **be** in the others.

1. I never found that book we were looking for. It ...*got*... lost when we moved house.
2. After the way he behaved last time he went to their house, it's unlikely he .... asked there again.
3. Naturally this vase is expensive. After all, it .... believed to be over three hundred years old.
4. I phoned to explain what had happened, but I .... cut off before I could finish.
5. There isn't any cheese left, I'm afraid. It .... eaten by the children.
6. He is a well-known expert on animal diseases and his opinions .... greatly respected.
7. My sister will be thrilled if her design .... chosen.
8. The book .... torn when the children started fighting over who should read it first.
9. Please don't touch anything on my desk. You .... supposed to answer the telephone, not tidy the office.
10. She was quite friendly at first, then she .... promoted and now she doesn't care about us any more.

112 Complete the second sentence so that it has a similar meaning to the first sentence.

1. It is said that house prices are too high.
   House prices ...*are said to be too high*... .

2. It is thought that the hospital is short of money.
   The hospital ....

3. It was alleged that the athlete had cheated.
   The athlete ....

4. It is reported that the prime minister is resigning.
   The prime minister ....

5. It is expected that the new sports stadium will be finished soon.
   The new sports stadium ....

6. It is generally considered that sixteen is too young to get married.
   Sixteen ....

7. It was thought that the book had been destroyed.
   The book ....

8. It is believed that the children had been hiding for two weeks.
   The children ....

The passive   Units 42–45

113 Look at these notes made by a journalist. Then complete the article she wrote for her newspaper. Use verbs in the correct passive form.

Kitchen
6 am visit market, choose vegetables and fruit
7 am plan menu
8 am unload meat
9 am cook staff breakfast
9.30 am make desserts
10 am wash vegetables
clean fish
put meat in oven
mix salads

Dining-room
11 am vacuum floor
lay tables
arrange flowers
12pm open doors
serve about 200 meals every lunchtime

EATING OUT with Eva Wolsey

It's exactly midday and I'm sitting in the Beverly Restaurant. Today I've been finding out just how much work goes on in a restaurant before the first customers arrive.

The staff have already done six hours work. The day began with a visit to the market where vegetables and fruit (1) _were chosen_. Back at the restaurant the menu (2) .... and then the day's delivery of meat (3) .... After that, breakfast (4) .... for the staff. But they didn't have long to eat it, because by 9.30 it was time for the desserts (5) .... After the vegetables (6) ...., the fish (7) .... and the meat (8) .... in the oven.

While this was happening in the kitchen, in the dining-room the floor (9) .... Since then, the tables (10) .... and the flowers (11) ...., so the dining-room looks fresh and pretty. In the last few minutes, salads (12) .... in the kitchen and in a moment the doors (13) .... In the next three hours, about two hundred meals (14) ....!

Have something done Unit 46

114 Tanya wants to rent a flat, but it needs some work before she can move in. She talks to the landlord and he agrees to her suggestions. Complete the conversation using **have** and the verbs in brackets.

TANYA: This flat is in a good place, but there are a few problems.
LANDLORD: Oh, really? What do you mean?
TANYA: The mirror is broken.
LANDLORD: (1) _I'll have it replaced._ (replace)
TANYA: There are marks on the carpet.
LANDLORD: (2) .... (clean)
TANYA: I don't like the colour of the walls.
LANDLORD: (3) .... (paint)
TANYA: All the furniture is in the wrong rooms.
LANDLORD: (4) .... (rearrange)
TANYA: One of the chairs is broken.
LANDLORD: (5) .... (mend)
TANYA: Several of the cupboards are full of old clothes.
LANDLORD: (6) .... (empty)
TANYA: The curtains are dirty.
LANDLORD: (7) .... (wash)
TANYA: Then I might rent the flat.

115 Rewrite the underlined words using **have something done**.

1 I didn't recognise Sheila because <u>the hairdresser's coloured her hair</u>.
   She's had her hair coloured.

2 My laptop was very slow, so <u>a friend is going to install a new operating system for me</u>.
   ....

3 Gaby's parents <u>are going to ask a painter to paint her portrait</u>.
   ....

4 Simon has made a lot of money, so <u>an architect's designed him a fine new house</u>.
   ....

5 This room gets hot when the sun shines, so <u>I'm employing someone to fit blinds on the windows.</u>
   ....

6 I heard that Mrs Green didn't trust her husband, so <u>she hired a detective to follow him</u>!
   ....

7 My sister had always been self-conscious about her nose, so she has decided to go to a clinic <u>for an operation which will straighten it</u>.
   ....

Questions

Units 49–50

116 Wilma Shriek the pop singer has just arrived in London from America. She's being interviewed by a journalist. Look at the journalist's notes and Wilma's answers. Then write the journalist's questions.

1. how long / be here?   *How long are you going to be here* ?   Two months.
2. be / first visit to this country?   *Is this your first visit* ?   No, it isn't.
3. when / be here before?   _____ ?   Five years ago.
4. why / come then?   _____ ?   For a holiday.
5. why / come this time?   _____ ?   To work.
6. do / a tour now?   _____ ?   Yeah, that's right.
7. how many cities / visit?   _____ ?   About twenty.
8. what / want to do after that?   _____ ?   Have a holiday.
9. have / message for your fans?   _____ ?   Yeah – come to our concerts and have a wild time.

117 Lucy works in a tourist information office and has to answer a lot of questions. Read her answers and complete the questions using the words in brackets.

1. TOURIST: Do you know *where the city maps are* ? (city maps)
   LUCY: Over there, on the other counter.

2. TOURIST: Can you tell me _____ ? (this guidebook)
   LUCY: £9.99.

3. TOURIST: Please could you tell me _____ ? (postcards)
   LUCY: They're on the third shelf, beside the window.

4. TOURIST: Do you happen to know _____ ? (the sports centre)
   LUCY: Yes, it closes at half past ten on weekdays and ten at weekends.

5. TOURIST: Could you explain _____ ? (this timetable)
   LUCY: It's quite simple. You find your destination on the left and read the times across the page.

6. TOURIST: I'd like to know _____ ? (free Internet access)
   LUCY: It's available in most city centre coffee shops and the public library.

7. TOURIST: Do you know _____ ? (the music festival)
   LUCY: The last weekend of July.

8. TOURIST: I can't remember _____ . (the castle)
   LUCY: It was built about 1500, so that makes it over 500 years old.

Questions

Units 49–50

118 Sonia Schmidt is phoning to book a hotel room. Complete the conversation by putting the words in the correct order. Do not change the form of the words.

SONIA: Hello. My name's Sonia Schmidt. I'd like to book a room for myself and my husband please, starting from next Thursday.

RECEPTIONIST: Certainly. (1) staying / how many nights / you / be / will
How many nights will you be staying ?

SONIA: Three, probably.

RECEPTIONIST: Yes, we have a double room on those nights.

SONIA: (2) available / is / one with a sea view
.... ?

RECEPTIONIST: Yes. By the way, (3) have / the special offer / about / are running / we / you / at the moment / heard
.... ?

SONIA: Oh, no.

RECEPTIONIST: It's four nights for the price of three (4) don't / take advantage / you / it / why / of
.... ?

SONIA: (5) have / for it / what / I / to do / to qualify / got
.... ?

RECEPTIONIST: Just make a definite booking today and let me have your credit card number. We won't use it until you leave.

SONIA: OK. (6) be / much / will / it / how / for bed and breakfast
.... ?

RECEPTIONIST: For three nights, £60 per person per night, plus the fourth night and breakfast free. So that's £360 all together.

SONIA: Yes. I think I'll do that. We can stay till Monday. (7) you / give / my credit card number / I / shall / now
.... ?

RECEPTIONIST: Yes please.

SONIA: 3434 8123 7650 9920.

RECEPTIONIST: Thank you very much. (8) would / to / me / you / email / like / confirmation of your reservation / you / to
.... ?

SONIA: Yes, please. To soniaschmidt@numail.com.

RECEPTIONIST: Thank you. We'll look forward to seeing you.

SONIA: Thank you, goodbye.

Questions • Units 49–50

119 Brian's doctor has advised him to join a Health Club. The instructor is going to help him to plan his fitness programme. Write the instructor's questions. Read the whole conversation before you begin.

INSTRUCTOR: OK, Brian. Let's find out how fit you are. (1) First of all, _how old are you_ ?
BRIAN: I'm thirty-two.
INSTRUCTOR: (2) And _____ ?
BRIAN: About seventy-five kilos.
INSTRUCTOR: (3) And _____ ?
BRIAN: One metre eighty.
INSTRUCTOR: (4) _____ ?
BRIAN: I work in a call centre for a bank.
INSTRUCTOR: Really? (5) So, _____ ?
BRIAN: Well, I take some exercise, but it's not regular.
INSTRUCTOR: (6) _____ ?
BRIAN: No, I haven't done any sport since I left school. I sometimes go for a walk on my day off if the weather's good.
INSTRUCTOR: I see. (7) _____ ?
BRIAN: Yes, I admit I do. Not more than a packet a day, though.
INSTRUCTOR: That's quite a lot, actually. (8) _____ ?
BRIAN: Well, I tried once, about a year ago, but then I started putting on weight. But my doctor says I must try again.
INSTRUCTOR: Well, we can give you some help with that too. It's really important, you know. Now if you'll come with me, I'm going to do a few checks and then we'll make a plan for you.
BRIAN: OK. Thanks.

120 There are mistakes in eight of these sentences. Correct the sentences where necessary. Write 'OK' if the sentence is already correct.

1 Have ever you been to Hawaii?   _Have you ever been_
2 What is this word mean?   _____
3 How much costs it to fly to Australia from here? _____
4 We can't remember where did we leave our car. _____
5 Had the film started when you turned the TV on? _____
6 Would you like to explain what is your problem? _____
7 How long did it you take to get here?   _____
8 Now I know why didn't you tell me what were you buying! _____
9 Can you tell me where the dictionaries are kept? _____
10 Why young people don't show more respect to the elderly? _____

English Grammar in Use Supplementary Exercises

Reported speech and questions

Units 47–50

121 Read the email. Then write what Angela actually said to Della.

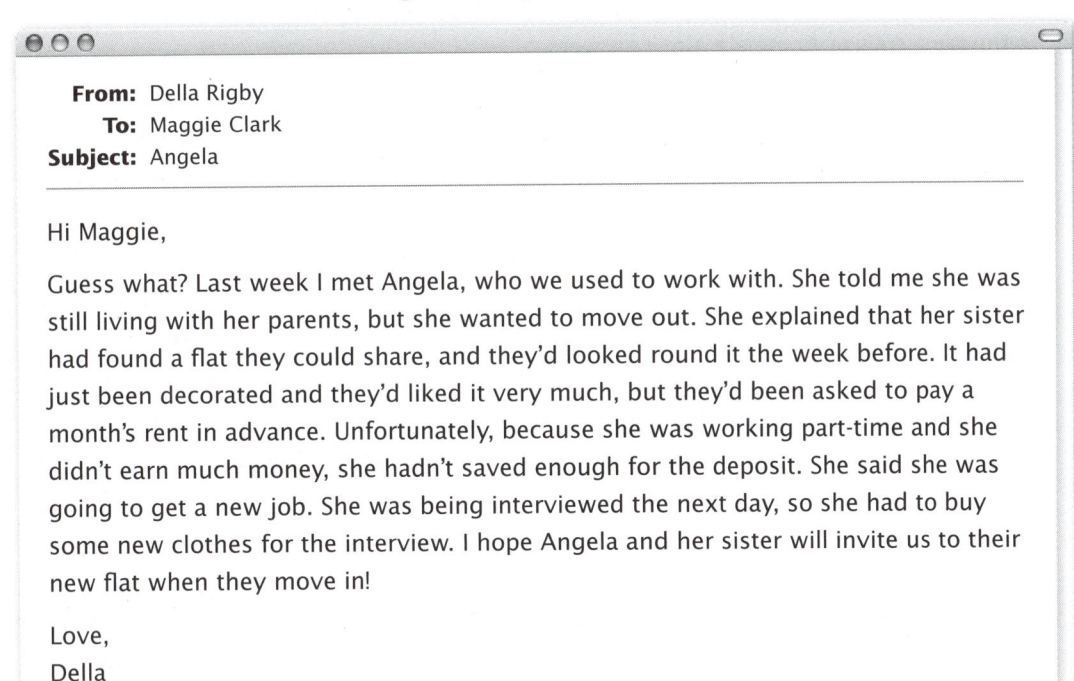

From: Della Rigby
To: Maggie Clark
Subject: Angela

Hi Maggie,

Guess what? Last week I met Angela, who we used to work with. She told me she was still living with her parents, but she wanted to move out. She explained that her sister had found a flat they could share, and they'd looked round it the week before. It had just been decorated and they'd liked it very much, but they'd been asked to pay a month's rent in advance. Unfortunately, because she was working part-time and she didn't earn much money, she hadn't saved enough for the deposit. She said she was going to get a new job. She was being interviewed the next day, so she had to buy some new clothes for the interview. I hope Angela and her sister will invite us to their new flat when they move in!

Love,
Della

ANGELA

> I'm still living with my parents, but

English Grammar in Use Supplementary Exercises 75

Reported speech and questions — Units 47–50

122 In Exercise 41, Alex, who wanted to go to an art college, was interviewed by one of the lecturers. A year later, his friend Charlie asked him about the interview, as he wanted to go to the same college. Complete Alex's answers.

CHARLIE: So, Alex, what was the interview like?
ALEX: Well, the interviewer started by asking me when I (1) _I'd left_ (leave) school. And then he wanted to know where I (2) .... (be) since then. I told him I (3) .... (have) several jobs. First I (4) .... (work) in a cafe for about a year because I (5) .... (need) to save a lot of money for travelling. Of course he asked me where I (6) .... (want) to go and when I told him, he asked whether I (7) .... (visit) all those places. I explained to him that I (8) .... (be) to Brazil and Peru, and I (9) .... (spend) some months in Turkey. He told me I (10) .... (be) very lucky. Then he asked if I (11) .... (bring) some work to show him and he looked at my work. He liked it, I think.

CHARLIE: Was that all?
ALEX: I think so. He asked me when I (12) .... (become) interested in painting and drawing, and I said that I (13) .... (think) I always (14) .... (be). Oh, yes, and he told me my work (15) .... (be) very good.

CHARLIE: I'm not surprised. It is good. I hope he'll like my stuff too.
ALEX: Oh, I think he will, actually.

123 Look back at your answers to Exercise 116. Complete the article which the journalist wrote a month after the interview with Wilma.

Last month I was lucky enough to interview Wilma Shriek when she was in this country. I asked her how long she (1) _was going to be_ here and she said two months, but actually she has already gone back to America. She told me it (2) .... her first visit because she (3) .... here five years before, for a holiday. She told me she (4) .... a tour. When I asked her how many cities she (5) ...., she thought about twenty. She said she (6) .... to have a holiday after the tour. She looked tired. But when I asked her whether she (7) .... a message for her fans, she told them (8) .... to the concerts and have a wild time. Well, it looks as though Wilma has had too many wild times, because her manager said last week that she is now resting!

English Grammar in Use Supplementary Exercises

Reported speech and questions

Units 47–50

124

John had a row with his girlfriend, Julie. His friend Mark tried to help them get back together and talked to Julie for John.

MARK: Julie, John's asked me to talk to you.
JULIE: I don't want to speak to him.
MARK: Look Julie, John's really upset.
JULIE: I'm upset too.
MARK: Will you just let me tell you his side of the story?
JULIE: I'm not interested. He promised to meet me at the restaurant, but he didn't turn up. I don't want to see him again.
MARK: But Julie, his car had broken down.
JULIE: So? I had my phone with me.
MARK: But that's the point. He tried to phone, but he couldn't get through.
JULIE: I don't believe he tried.
MARK: Yes, he did. His phone wasn't working, so he came to my flat and tried on my landline. Do you believe me?
JULIE: OK, I'll talk to him. Listen, I'm going to be late for work. I'll meet him at six o'clock in the square.
MARK: Thanks, Julie. He'll be really happy. And I promise he'll be there.

Complete the conversation Mark had later with John.

JOHN: What did Julie say?
MARK: She said she (1) *didn't want to speak to you*.
JOHN: Well, what did she say when you told her I was really upset?
MARK: She said she (2) .... too, so I asked her to let me explain your side of the story. She said she (3) .... You (4) .... to meet her at the restaurant, but you (5) .... She said she (6) .... again.
JOHN: Did you explain about the car?
MARK: Yes, and she said she (7) .... her phone with her. So I explained you couldn't get through, but she said she (8) .... you (9) .... Then I told her you (10) .... to my flat and (11) .... on my landline. I asked her (12) .... me. I think she did. Anyway, she said she (13) .... to you. Then she said she (14) .... late for work, so we had to finish. You have to meet her in the square at six o'clock.
JOHN: Thanks, Mark. I really appreciate what you've done for me.
MARK: That's OK. Just don't be late this evening.

Reported speech and questions — Units 47–50

125 You've just arrived at the Great Bay Hotel for a holiday. It's not the same as your travel agent told you it would be. Look at your travel agent's website and complete the email you send to the travel agent.

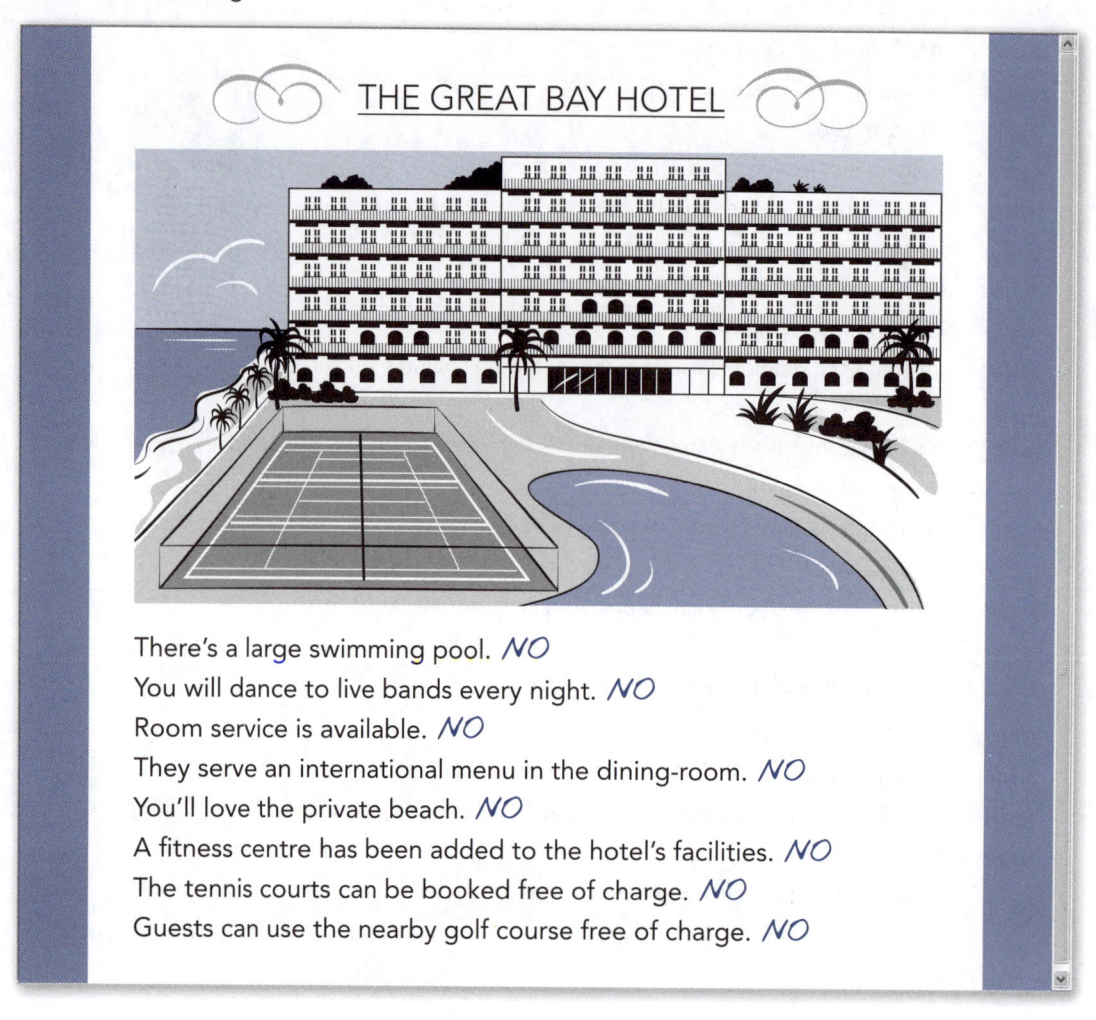

THE GREAT BAY HOTEL

There's a large swimming pool. *NO*
You will dance to live bands every night. *NO*
Room service is available. *NO*
They serve an international menu in the dining-room. *NO*
You'll love the private beach. *NO*
A fitness centre has been added to the hotel's facilities. *NO*
The tennis courts can be booked free of charge. *NO*
Guests can use the nearby golf course free of charge. *NO*

To: Mr Smiley, Sunways Travel Agency

I am very disappointed because the Great Bay Hotel is quite different from what you told us. You said there *was a large swimming pool* and that we

....

You also said ....

The website said ....

You told us ....

In fact, none of these facilities is available. Please arrange for us to be transferred to a better hotel immediately.

78 English Grammar in Use Supplementary Exercises

Reported speech and questions

Units 47–50

126 Anna has just met the singer Colin Boyle. (You may remember him from Exercise 16.) She is telling Ian, about the meeting. Ian wants to know exactly what Colin said to Anna and what she said to him.

IAN: Well, what was he like? Was he friendly? What did he say?
ANNA: He was really friendly. (1) <u>He asked me who I was</u>.
IAN: Then what?
ANNA: (2) <u>He asked me where I came from</u>.
IAN: And what did you say?
ANNA: (3) <u>I told him I came from Dublin</u>, of course. Then (4) <u>he said that was where he was born too</u>. Then (5) <u>I told him I'd been a fan of his for ages</u> and (6) <u>he said that was very good to hear</u>. Then (7) <u>he asked whether I was going to the concert tonight</u>. So (8) <u>I told him we wanted to, but we hadn't been able to get tickets</u>. (9) <u>He asked if the tickets were sold out</u>, and (10) <u>I told him they'd sold all but the most expensive ones and we couldn't afford those</u>.
IAN: And did he give you some tickets?
ANNA: No, he didn't. But (11) <u>he asked the concert hall manager if we could have some at the cheaper price</u>. And the manager said 'Yes'!

Now write exactly what Anna and Colin said.

1 Colin asked: *Who are you?*
2 Colin asked: ....
3 Anna said: ....
4 Colin said: ....
5 Anna said: ....
6 Colin said: ....
7 Colin asked: ....
8 Anna said: ....
9 Colin asked: ....
10 Anna said: ....
11 Colin asked the concert hall manager: ....

127 Imagine that when you were on holiday last year you met someone famous. This could be a musician, a film star, a sportsman or woman, a politician, etc. Look at what Anna told Ian in Exercise 126 and write an email to a friend about the conversation you had.

From:
To:
Subject:
Hi!
I never told you that when I was on holiday last year I met ....

English Grammar in Use Supplementary Exercises

Reported speech and questions — Units 47–50

128 Rewrite the sentences beginning in the way shown.

1 'Where are you going?' asked Tom.
   Tom asked (me) where I was going.

2 'Where are you going to spend the holiday?' asked Mike.
   Mike asked ....

3 'What will you do when you leave school?' asked Jennifer.
   Jennifer asked ....

4 'How did you know my name?' the journalist asked the security guard.
   The journalist wanted to know ....

5 'Do you have an appointment?' asked the clerk.
   The clerk asked ....

6 'Have you seen the blue memory stick?' Bernard asked his wife.
   Bernard wondered ....

7 'Why didn't Isobel phone me?' asked her brother.
   Isobel's brother wanted to know ....

8 'Will you carry my laptop for me please, Rosemary?' Richard asked.
   Richard asked ....

9 'When can I see the doctor?' Charles asked the receptionist.
   Charles asked ....

129 Complete the sentences with the correct form of say or tell.

1 *Did you tell* (you) your brother the truth about that money?
2 What .... (you) to Wendy last night? She looks terribly upset this morning.
3 Is something wrong? Can you .... me about it?
4 My English teacher keeps asking me .... the class a joke from my country, but I can't think of any suitable ones!
5 If I asked you to marry me, what .... (you)?
6 I never know what .... to people when they pay me a compliment.
7 Don't worry, I'm sure the boys are fine. Anyway, I .... them to call me if they had any problems.
8 I'll never speak to him again after all the lies he .... me last weekend.
9 If I were you, I .... (not) anything about your problems now.
10 Promise you .... (not) anything to my girlfriend. She'll be furious if she finds out what I've done.
11 I .... (already) you, I don't know where your phone is.
12 Please .... you'll forgive me. I'm really sorry for all the trouble I've caused.
13 I'm ready to serve the meal. Can you .... the children to go and wash their hands, please?

Reported speech and questions

Units 47–50

130

Complete the email with the correct form of **say** or **tell**.

> From: Neville Cripps
> To: Stephanie Peters
> Subject: Talk with my dad
>
> Hello Stephanie,
>
> I must (1) _tell_ you about the talk I had with my dad last weekend. We talked for hours and I (2) _____ him all about the plans we've made for our business. At first, he wasn't very interested, he (3) _____ he didn't think we were old enough to run a business. But then I (4) _____ him that we had already talked to a small business adviser, and she (5) _____ that the plan seemed realistic. She agreed that all we need is a small loan at a reasonable rate.
>
> So after that he sat down and asked me (6) _____ him exactly how much money we'd need to start with, and how long for. Eventually he (7) _____ to me, 'OK, it's a good plan. (8) _____ Stephanie that I'll lend you the money to get started.' Honestly, I couldn't believe he (9) _____ it! Isn't it great? I'm really looking forward to seeing you next week so we can talk to him together and get things going.
>
> All the best,
> Neville

131

There are mistakes in four of these sentences. Correct the sentences where necessary. Write 'OK' if the sentence is already correct.

1 Joan said she had been very happy in her new job and liked her new boss better than her old one.   _said she was very happy_
2 Michael explained that he couldn't come to the party because he was working that evening.   _____
3 We had a great evening with Janet. She was saying us about her fascinating trip to Kenya.   _____
4 I'm sorry to bother you, but you said to call if I was worried.   _____
5 We were disappointed when the receptionist told that the hotel was fully booked that week.   _____
6 The museum guard asked the visitors to not touch the exhibits.   _____
7 The tour guide explained that the Severn is the longest river in England.   _____

–ing and infinitive

Units 53–58

132 Put the verbs into the correct form: –ing or infinitive.

1. I don't get on with the new boss, so I've asked ____to be transferred____ (transfer) to another branch of the company.

2. Please stop ____interrupting____ (interrupt) me when I'm explaining something to you. You can ask questions at the end.

3. He admits _____ (enter) the house, but he says he didn't take anything.

4. What a dreadful man! Can you imagine _____ (live) with him?

5. I've forgotten _____ (bring) my briefcase with me. I'll have to go back for it.

6. We had hoped _____ (live) in our new house by now, but the builders are still working on it.

7. I don't mind _____ (work) late if it will help at all.

8. You'll just have to find a job. I simply can't afford _____ (support) you any longer.

English Grammar in Use Supplementary Exercises

–ing and infinitive

Units 53–58

133
Put the verbs into the correct form: –ing or infinitive.

CYCLIST ABANDONS 24 HR RIDE

For the second time, Andrew Spicer, the local cycling star, has decided (1) _to give up_ (give up) the attempt (2) .... (ride) his bike non-stop for twenty-four hours. His decision came after poor weather conditions had caused him to postpone (3) .... (set off) for several hours. His first attempt had also ended in failure, when he appeared (4) .... (lose) control of his bicycle as he attempted to avoid (5) .... (hit) a small child and crashed into a wall. He says that he has not yet decided whether (6) .... (try) one more time, but denies (7) .... (lose) interest in the project. 'I've promised (8) .... (raise) money for the local hospital,' he explained. 'They deserve help. I shall do what I can if I manage (9) .... (find) the time.'

134
Complete the conversations with suitable verbs in the correct form: –ing or infinitive.

A ANN: What are you doing this weekend?
BILL: I'm hoping (1) _to visit_ my brother at his university if I can.
ANN: I thought you went to see him last weekend.
BILL: No, I was planning (2) .... him then, but he emailed me and suggested (3) .... the visit for a week because he hadn't finished (4) .... his thesis. Now he's done it, we can celebrate.

B CILLA: Can you help me get these packages posted today? One of our main customers has said he'll consider (5) .... to another supplier if we don't improve our delivery times.
DAVE: Have we been failing (6) .... on time? I didn't know that.
CILLA: Apparently someone forgot (7) .... one order last month. So I agreed (8) .... them myself this time – we can't risk (9) .... such an important customer.

C JACK: Oh dear, here's another email from Peter.
SEAN: Why does he keep (10) .... you?
JACK: He wants me to join his basketball team. He's offered (11) .... me fix my car if I agree (12) .... them. The trouble is, I'd have to go to a lot of training sessions and I haven't got time. And I can fix the car by myself.
SEAN: Well, you'll just have to find a way to say no. You can't avoid (13) .... to him forever.

–ing and infinitive   Units 53–58

135 Complete the sentences using –ing or infinitive.

1. Terry wanted Chris _to help him_.
2. The coach ordered _____.
3. The gangsters forced _____.
4. Laura regretted _____.
5. Felicity made _____.
6. John tried _____.
7. The car needed _____.
8. Jim helped _____.

–ing and infinitive   Units 53–58

136 Complete the conversations with the correct form of the verbs and any other words you need.

A PAT: Who should I ask if I want a day off?
MICK: It doesn't really matter, except I'd advise (1) _you not to ask_ (not / ask) the assistant manager. He can be very rude sometimes.
PAT: Oh, I don't mind (2) _____ (shout) at by him. He threatened (3) _____ (sack) me last week, but he apologised very politely later.

B SUE: I don't trust the new director of marketing.
JILL: Why not?
SUE: Well, she claims (4) _____ (work) in several different countries before she came here. But when I asked her where exactly, she kept (5) _____ (change) the subject. I was wondering whether (6) _____ (say) something to the boss.
JILL: Perhaps she's just shy. Why don't we go on (7) _____ (be) friendly for a few more days and see how she behaves?
SUE: OK. I'd hate (8) _____ (get) someone into trouble for nothing.

C ANDY: I don't know what to do about Gemma. She's so difficult to work with. She keeps forgetting (9) _____ (pass) on important messages and she won't let me (10) _____ (help) her when she's busy.
JOAN: Have you actually talked to her about all this?
ANDY: That's part of the problem. I've tried (11) _____ (discuss) the problem with her, but she always says she's too busy to stop and talk. I've even tried (12) _____ (ask) her to have lunch with me, but she doesn't want to.
JOAN: I think I'd better have a chat with her. How long has she been like this?
ANDY: Oh, it's several weeks now.
JOAN: Well, I'd really like (13) _____ (know) about the problem earlier. Never mind, I'll see what I can do.
ANDY: Thanks very much.

137 Complete the sentences with your own ideas. Use –ing or the infinitive.

1 I often help _to prepare lunch at weekends_ .
2 I learnt _____ at the age of _____ .
3 I can't help _____ when I see someone being treated unfairly.
4 I don't mind _____ , but I hate _____ .
5 I sometimes pretend _____ when really I'm just daydreaming.
6 I always encourage _____ which I have enjoyed reading myself.
7 I remember _____ when I was a small child.
8 I enjoy _____ even though I'm not very good at it.
9 I expect _____ by the end of next year.
10 I've given up _____ .

Prepositions and expressions + –ing

Units 60, 63

138 Match the beginning of each sentence with the most suitable ending.

How to study efficiently

1 Begin by
2 Be realistic: there's no point in
3 Find a quiet place where you can work without
4 If possible, use this place only for
5 Check you have everything you need before
6 This means you won't waste time
7 Encourage yourself by

a making plans you can't possibly keep.
b ~~making a list of what you have to do.~~
c studying.
d marking each topic on your list as you complete it.
e jumping up to fetch things every five minutes.
f being interrupted.
g starting work.

1 b
2 ....
3 ....
4 ....
5 ....
6 ....
7 ....

139 Use the notes to complete the advice below. Use –ing and a preposition if necessary.

> 1 Read through the exam paper carefully.
> 2 Check the instructions.
> 3 Don't spend too long on one question.
> 4 Don't try to see how your friends are getting on.
> 5 Allow time to check all your answers.
> 6 Cheats rarely do well in the long run.

How to take exams

1 Begin _by reading through the exam paper carefully_.
2 Make sure you know exactly what to do ....
3 There's no point ....
4 Don't waste time ....
5 Avoid careless mistakes ....
6 It's rarely worth ....

140 Complete the pieces of advice. Use –ing and your own ideas.

1 It's rude to borrow people's things without _asking their permission first_ .
2 You should eat a healthy diet instead of ....
3 You won't get rich by ....
4 You must always thank people for ....
5 You shouldn't insist on ....
6 It's dangerous to go walking in the mountains without ....
7 It's good manners to apologise for ....
8 You should check delivery charges before ....

I'm used to doing and I used to do

141 Put the verbs into the correct form.

Dear Ruth,

Thanks very much for the lovely present you sent for Laurie. It was very kind of you. You say in your note that you haven't got used to (1) _being_ (be) an aunt yet. I used to (2) _think_ (think) that becoming a father wouldn't change me. I was wrong, of course! Life will never be the same again. We never used to (3) _____ (go) to bed before midnight, but now we're asleep by ten because we've had to get used to (4) _____ (wake) up at five o'clock. Actually, in a way, that's good. I always used to (5) _____ (arrive) late at the office, but since Laurie was born my colleagues have got used to (6) _____ (find) me hard at work by the time they arrive!

I should say, though, it hasn't been so easy for Jenny. At first she found it very hard on her own with Laurie. She wasn't used to (7) _____ (spend) all day alone with a baby. But now she's got to know a neighbour who also has a young baby and that helps. She used to (8) _____ (say) she'd go back to work when Laurie was six months, but now she's used to (9) _____ (be) at home she's beginning to enjoy herself, so she may wait until Laurie is a bit older.

Anyway, try to come and see us soon while Laurie is still small.

All the best,
Dennis

To ... and preposition + –ing
(Afraid to do and afraid of doing)

Units 65–66

142

Complete the conversations. Use a preposition + –ing or the infinitive.

A Sid and Tom are walking through the town centre.

SID: Look, there's Angela. Isn't she stunning?
TOM: She's all right. You really fancy her, don't you?
SID: Yeah. I often dream (1) _about taking_ (take) her out, but I'm afraid (2) _to ask_ (ask) her.
TOM: Why?
SID: Well, I suppose I'm afraid (3) .... (look) like a fool if she refuses.
TOM: If you like her so much, you shouldn't be afraid (4) .... (risk) it. Anyway, I'm sure she won't refuse.
SID: You think so?
TOM: Yeah, go on, why don't you text her?
SID: OK, I'll do it now.
TOM: It's lucky for me that I've succeeded (5) .... (persuade) you.
SID: Why's that?
TOM: I just happen to know she fancies you. I told her I'd get you to contact her and she's looking forward (6) .... (hear) from you!

B Brian and Phil are at work.

BRIAN: Good morning Phil, could we have a word in my office?
PHIL: Of course.
BRIAN: I'm sorry (7) .... (have) to say this, but I'm afraid you failed (8) .... (achieve) high enough sales to earn a bonus this month. I suppose the bad weather kept the customers away?
PHIL: Yes, I guess so. I'm very sorry (9) .... (let) you down this time.
BRIAN: OK, I'm sure you'll make it up soon. I'm thinking (10) .... (send) one or two junior sales staff on a course next month. Would you be interested (11) .... (go)?
PHIL: Yes, I would be. Thank you.
BRIAN: Good. I'll put your name on the list.

C Joanna has phoned Katie.

JOANNA: I'm sorry (12) .... (forget) your birthday last week.
KATIE: That's OK. You were in the middle of your exams. You're allowed (13) .... (forget) people's birthdays on exam days!
JOANNA: That shouldn't have prevented me (14) .... (send) you a card. Did you get some from the family?
KATIE: Well, Mum was the only one (15) .... (remember).
JOANNA: Well, she's not likely (16) .... (forget), is she?
KATIE: No, I suppose you're right.

Verb forms: review

143 Put the verbs in the correct form. Can you solve this detective puzzle?

Trevor Stern was not a popular man, in spite of his wealth. He (1) _lived_ (live) in a large house about a mile outside the village of Prenton. When he (2) _was found_ (find) dead in his study, no-one (3) _cried_ (cry), not even his only daughter. It was soon clear that he (4) .... (murder).

Detective Inspector Blackledge took statements from his widow Delia, his fifteen-year-old daughter Lucy, his business partner Gerald Brook, and his doctor.

Delia gave her statement first.

DELIA

I (5) .... (not / love) my husband, he was a cold and selfish man. But I (6) .... (not / murder) him, either. After dinner last night he said he (7) .... (want) to check some business papers in his study. He (8) .... (have) a meeting with Gerald, his business partner, the next morning. He (9) .... (ask) for some tea. That was about nine o'clock. I (10) .... (watch) a rather exciting film, so I (11) .... (tell) Lucy to take it to him.

At quarter past nine Doctor Emerson (12) .... (call). I (13) .... (notice) the time because we (14) .... (expect) him to come earlier. I (15) .... (answer) the front door bell. Trevor (16) .... (shout) in his study. He and Lucy (17) .... (obviously / have) a serious row. So I (18) .... (take) the doctor into the sitting-room for a moment. Then Trevor stopped (19) .... (shout). I guessed Lucy (20) .... (go) out by the back door. Doctor Emerson went to the study. I think he wanted to persuade Trevor (21) .... (go) into hospital for some tests, but Trevor (22) .... (not / want) to go.

I (23) .... (hear) my husband shouting again several times over the next twenty minutes. He called Emerson an ignorant country doctor and later he said something like, 'There's nothing you can do!' I think Lucy (24) .... (come) back into the house while the doctor (25) .... (still / talk) to Trevor. I (26) .... (hear) the front door bang during a moment of quiet when Trevor (27) .... (not / shout). I was tired and fed up, and went to my bedroom soon after that. My sister (28) .... (phone) and we (29) .... (talk) for ages. I (30) .... (tell) her I (31) .... (decide) to leave Trevor.

Verb forms: review

LUCY

Mum (32) .... (watch) a stupid film after dinner, so she made me (33) .... (take) Dad's tea into his study. It was about nine o'clock. He was in a really mean mood. He shouted at me because I (34) .... (spill) a few drops of tea on his desk while I (35) .... (pour) it. I (36) .... (not / want) to watch the film with Mum, so I (37) .... (creep) out of the house by the back door. I (38) .... (decide) to go down to the village and text my boyfriend Alan to meet me outside his house. I (39) .... (never / tell) Mum or Dad when I (40) .... (see) him. Especially yesterday, because Dad and I (41) .... (have) a stupid argument about Alan the day before.

It (42) .... (usually / take) quarter of an hour to walk to the village. Perhaps it (43) .... (take) less time last night. I can't prove I (44) .... (go) to the village. No-one (45) .... (see) me while I (46) .... (walk) there. I (47) .... (see) Gerald, that's Dad's business partner. He (48) .... (stand) near the window in his sitting-room. He (49) .... (not / see) me though, because it was dark outside. He (50) .... (talk) on the phone, I think. Alan (51) .... (not / answer) my text by the time I (52) .... (reach) his house. Then I (53) .... (remember) he (54) .... (play) in a concert that evening. So I (55) .... (walk) home again. I (56) .... (meet) Gerald just before I (57) .... (reach) our house. He (58) .... (look) for his dog. That was about twenty to ten. I came in by the back door as quietly as possible and went to bed. I didn't want to see my parents again that evening.

DOCTOR EMERSON

I (59) .... (call) at the Sterns' house at 9.15. I (60) .... (be) rather later than I (61) .... (plan) to be because I (62) .... (visit) another patient. When Mrs Stern (63) .... (let) me into the house, she (64) .... (seem) rather embarrassed and (65) .... (show) me into the sitting-room. I could hear Trevor Stern (66) .... (shout) at someone in his study. Mrs Stern said something about teenage girls and that they (67) .... (have) problems with Lucy. Well, the shouting (68) .... (stop) almost immediately, so I (69) .... (go) to his study. Lucy (70) .... (already / leave) the room before I (71) .... (get) there. I tried (72) .... (explain) to Trevor why he needed (73) .... (have) these hospital tests, but he (74) .... (not / listen). He said I (75) .... (be) an ignorant country doctor who (76) .... (not / know) what he (77) .... (talk) about. I (78) .... (realise) it was no use (79) .... (argue) with him, so I (80) .... (leave) after only a few minutes. I was quite angry actually. I let myself out of the house without (81) .... (see) Lucy or Mrs Stern.

Verb forms: review

Yes, Trevor was my business partner. We (82) .... (not / be) really friends. Yes, my house (83) .... (be) just round the corner from the Sterns'. I (84) .... (live) here for two years now. I (85) .... (have) a little cottage in the village. But I (86) .... (buy) this house when I started (87) .... (earn) a lot of money.

GERALD

I can't really tell you very much about the night Trevor died. I took my dog for a long walk that evening. I (88) .... (go) up on the hills, away from the village. Then the stupid dog (89) .... (run) after a rabbit or something and I (90) .... (lose) him in the dark. I (91) .... (look) for him when I (92) .... (meet) Lucy, as a matter of fact. She (93) .... (walk) up the road towards their house. She (94) .... (seem) rather upset. I told her I (95) .... (look) for my dog, but she said she (96) .... (not / see) it. She (97) .... (go) into her house and I (98) .... (find) the dog a few minutes afterwards. I was back home by just after quarter to ten.

Detective Inspector Blackledge showed the statements to her colleague, Sergeant Ross.

BLACKLEDGE: Well, Ross. What do you think? Who killed Stern?

ROSS: I don't know. It (99) .... (not / be) his wife. She (100) .... (not / even / go) into the study.

BLACKLEDGE: But she admits she didn't love him. Do you think she's in love with the doctor?

ROSS: It's possible. And perhaps Trevor Stern (101) .... (find out). But we know the doctor was at the hospital by ten o'clock that night. And that's at least half an hour from the Sterns' house.

BLACKLEDGE: But that (102) .... (mean) he (103) .... (leave) the Sterns' house before half past nine.

ROSS: Exactly. Also, Delia Stern told her sister she (104) .... (leave) her husband. She didn't need (105) .... (murder) him.

BLACKLEDGE: Yes, and there's something about Lucy's story which doesn't quite fit. Let's see, what did Gerald Brook say?

ROSS: That's it! Lucy (106) .... (not / walk) to the village and back if he (107) .... (meet) her at twenty to ten. She (108) .... (still / shout at) by her father at 9.15.

BLACKLEDGE: But look at all the statements. The times don't fit.

ROSS: Neither do the facts. Someone (109) .... (tell) lies.

BLACKLEDGE: I think it's time we (110) .... (make) an arrest.

Who did they arrest? See page 120.

English Grammar in Use Supplementary Exercises

Countable and uncountable

Units 69–70

144 Some of these sentences need **a/an**. Correct the sentences where necessary.

1 Joanna eats apple every morning.   *an apple*
2 Peter doesn't like milk in his tea.   *OK*
3 Katie rarely has biscuit with her coffee.
4 George normally eats meat for dinner.
5 Brian usually has omelette for lunch.
6 Margaret never drinks beer.

145 Lizzie is training to run in a marathon. Every day she writes down how far she runs and what she eats. Look at the pictures of what she ate today and complete what she wrote, using **a/an** where necessary.

BREAKFAST   LUNCH   DINNER

Monday
I ran 15 km. I had (1) *cereal* and (2) .... for breakfast. At lunchtime I ate (3) .... and (4) .... For dinner I had (5) .... and (6) .... , then (7) .... with (8) .... , followed by (9) ....

146 Do you have a healthy lifestyle? Doctors advise us to take regular exercise and to eat at least five portions of fruit or vegetables every day. Look at what Lizzie wrote. Write down what you ate yesterday.

DIARY   Date:

English Grammar in Use Supplementary Exercises

Countable and uncountable

Units 69–70

147 There are mistakes in seven of these sentences. Correct the sentences where necessary. Write 'OK' if the sentence is already correct.

1 You need a permission from your teacher to use this software. — you need permission
2 We're looking for a flat to rent. — OK
3 I'm late because the traffics are awful. —
4 He was asked to leave the club because of a bad behaviour. —
5 I phoned my brother to wish him good luck in the exam. —
6 It's a pity Rebecca had her hairs cut so short. —
7 I like the flat but the furnitures are very old-fashioned. —
8 As an old friend, may I give you an advice? —
9 We need to get up-to-date information about flight times. —
10 Cycling home in the rain wasn't pleasant experience! —

148 Complete the conversation with the words from the box. Sometimes you need the plural (–s). Use some of the words more than once.

| case | day | experience | luggage | paper | room | scenery | weather | view |

Mary and Liz are about to go on holiday together. Mary has come to collect Liz in her car.

MARY: Hello, Liz, are you ready?

LIZ: Yes, just about. All my (1) _luggage_ is here. I hope I haven't got too many (2) _cases_ .

MARY: Don't worry. There's plenty of (3) .... in the car.

LIZ: Oh, good. I've packed rather a lot of things. I haven't had much (4) .... of travelling in the mountains, so I wasn't sure what to bring.

MARY: As long as you've got some warm sweaters for the evenings, and a good raincoat, you should be OK. The (5) .... in the mountains is wonderful, but the (6) .... can change very suddenly.

LIZ: Well, we've got a lovely (7) .... to start with.

MARY: You're right there. And I'm sure you'll like our (8) .... at the hotel, because they've promised me the ones I had last year when I was with my brother. Did you pack the guidebook, by the way?

LIZ: Yes, and I packed some (9) .... so we can do some drawing.

MARY: That's a good idea. It'd be nice to keep some sort of diary too.

LIZ: Yes. We might make an album afterwards, with words and pictures. And I'm sure I'm going to have some great (10) .... to write about.

MARY: Well, the (11) .... are like nothing you've ever seen. And there's always music or something in one of the villages every evening. We'll buy the local (12) .... when we get there and find out what's going on.

LIZ: Well, I'm ready.

MARY: OK, let's go!

English Grammar in Use Supplementary Exercises

A/an, some and the

149 Complete the description with **a/an**, **some** or **the**.

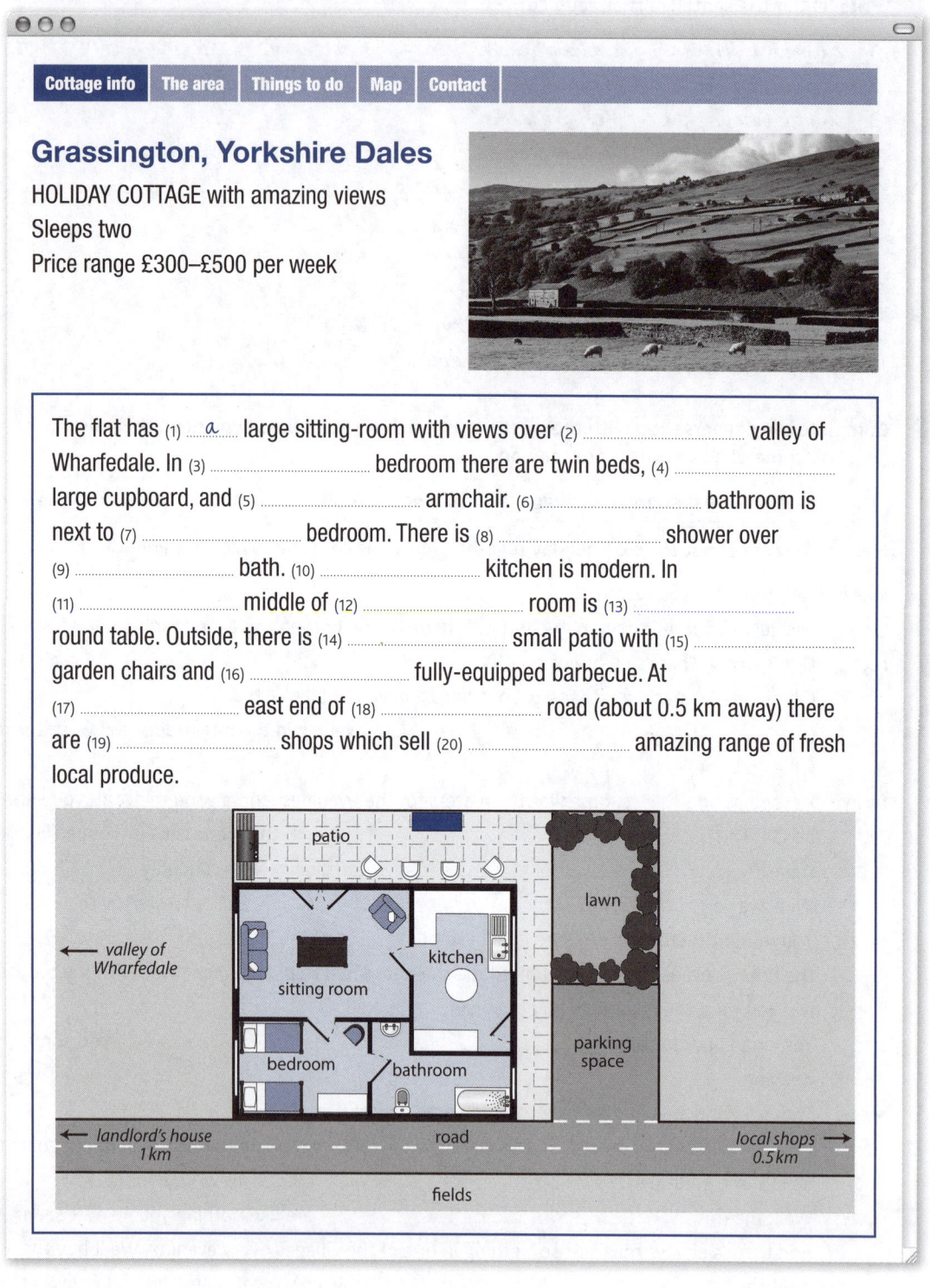

Cottage info | The area | Things to do | Map | Contact

Grassington, Yorkshire Dales
HOLIDAY COTTAGE with amazing views
Sleeps two
Price range £300–£500 per week

The flat has (1) _a_ large sitting-room with views over (2) _____ valley of Wharfedale. In (3) _____ bedroom there are twin beds, (4) _____ large cupboard, and (5) _____ armchair. (6) _____ bathroom is next to (7) _____ bedroom. There is (8) _____ shower over (9) _____ bath. (10) _____ kitchen is modern. In (11) _____ middle of (12) _____ room is (13) _____ round table. Outside, there is (14) _____ small patio with (15) _____ garden chairs and (16) _____ fully-equipped barbecue. At (17) _____ east end of (18) _____ road (about 0.5 km away) there are (19) _____ shops which sell (20) _____ amazing range of fresh local produce.

Now look at the plan of the flat and write two more sentences of your own about the flat.

21 ....
22 ....

English Grammar in Use Supplementary Exercises

A/an, some and the

Units 71–72

150 Write a description of your home or somewhere you have stayed on holiday. Use about 80 words.

....
....
....
....
....

151 Put in **a/an** or **the**.

Tina wants to buy a car. She has come to see Ryan, who is trying to sell his.

TINA: So, you don't say much in your advert. Is this (1) ...*an*... old car?
RYAN: Not very old. Come and have a look at it.
TINA: Were you (2) .... first owner?
RYAN: No, I got it two years ago.
TINA: Have you driven it a lot?
RYAN: Well, I drive to my office in (3) .... city centre five days (4) .... week, but I don't use it much at weekends.
TINA: I see. Now, the thing is, I'm (5) .... doctor. I've just started work at (6) .... hospital in Hills Road. I'm on call a lot of the time and I have to find (7) .... car which is really reliable. (8) .... car I used to have was always breaking down and giving me problems.
RYAN: Oh, this one's very good. It may not be (9) .... fastest car around, but it always gets there eventually. And it's got (10) .... new set of tyres.
TINA: Right. It's good to know that. Can I go for (11) .... test drive?
RYAN: Um, actually, that's not possible right now.
TINA: Why not?
RYAN: Well, basically, I'm afraid it won't start. You see, (12) .... battery is flat.

English Grammar in Use Supplementary Exercises

The

Units 73–78

152

Put in **the** where necessary. If **the** is not necessary, leave the space empty (–).

Portrait of a family: (1) ...**The**... Campbells

There are seven people in this family. (2) ...**The**... children are Sandra, aged sixteen, Craig aged nineteen, and (3) ...**–**... young twins, Michelle and Ryan, who are nearly seven. Their parents are Jack and Sylvia. (4) .... other adult is Irina, Sylvia's mother. They live in Brisbane, on (5) .... east coast of Queensland, Australia.

On (6) .... weekday mornings everyone gets up early. Jack Walsh works for a company which makes (7) .... paper. He leaves at seven o'clock, to avoid (8) .... rush hour, and perhaps to avoid having breakfast with (9) .... twins, who are very noisy. Sandra catches (10) .... school bus at seven-fifty. Craig is at (11) .... art school, studying photography. He lives away from (12) .... home during term-time, so he avoids (13) .... noise too.

Ryan and Michelle don't go to (14) .... school by (15) .... bus because their school is just down (16) .... road from their house. After school, their grandmother looks after them as their parents are at (17) .... work until six o'clock. Sylvia works at (18) .... Modern Art Gallery which is beside (19) .... River Brisbane in (20) .... city centre.

153

Write a similar description of a family you know or a famous family.

....
....
....
....
....

154

Read these news items carefully and cross out **the** where it is not necessary.

PM TOUR The Prime Minister leaves this morning for a tour of the Far East. He will visit ~~the~~ Singapore and the Malaysia and then go to the Philippines, for a conference about the global warming.

ROYAL VISIT The King Juan Carlos of the Spain arrives today for a short visit to the United Kingdom. After lunch with the Queen at the Windsor Castle, he will open an exhibition at the National Gallery in the Trafalgar Square and in the evening he will have talks with the businessmen.

RAIL CRASH An accident has closed the main railway line between London and Southampton. Several people were hurt when a train hit a bridge. The injured have been taken to the Southampton Hospital. For the information phone the police on 01273 01023.

Quantifiers and pronouns

Units 86–91

155 While you were on holiday, some thieves stole your wallet. You saw them, but they got away. Complete the description you gave to the police.

1. All *of them had fair hair*.
2. None *of them was older than forty*.
3. Both *(of) the men were wearing T-shirts*.
4. One *of the men had a shoulder bag*.
5. All ....
6. None ....
7. Both ....
8. Both ....
9. Both ....
10. Neither ....
11. Neither ....
12. One ....

156 Use the words in the first box to make true statements about the people in the second box.

(a) few (of)   all (of)   both (of)   lots (of)   most (of)
neither of   none of   one of   some (of)

bands   classmates   cousins   doctors   friends   grandfathers
neighbours   parents   politicians   relatives   students

1. *Most of the students in my class like rock music.*
2. *Both my grandfathers were farmers.*
3. *One of the bands I like is Kings of Leon.*
4. *Few of my friends wear high-heeled shoes.*
5. ....
6. ....
7. ....
8. ....
9. ....

English Grammar in Use Supplementary Exercises

Quantifiers and pronouns

Units 86–91

157

Complete the sentences using words from the box.

| a few (of) | all (of) | any (of) | each (of) | few (of) |
| half (of) | most (of) | much (of) | none (of) | |

1 It is widely believed that ...all... human beings are descended from one common ancestor.
2 When Jill decided to sell her car, she phoned round her friends. But .... them wanted to buy it, so she put an ad in the paper.
3 Do .... your colleagues give you birthday presents?
4 When my rich uncle died, he left .... his fortune to his cat and the other half to a distant cousin! We had never expected to receive .... it, but we were disappointed that he hadn't left .... it to us.
5 I think .... children enjoy going to funfairs, although I know .... who are frightened of the big rides.
6 We'll have to work quickly because I haven't got .... time.
7 Before mixing the cake, weigh .... ingredient precisely.
8 I'll have to buy a new tie. .... the ones I've got matches this jacket.
9 .... people enjoy housework, and I'm not one of them.
10 Brett lost his wallet, so he phoned .... the shops he'd visited. But he got the same answer from .... place. Unfortunately, ... their staff had found it.

158

There are mistakes in all these sentences. Correct the sentences.

1 He shouted at <u>all of students</u> although most of us had done nothing wrong. — <u>all of the students</u>
2 You can't borrow money from me because I have no.
3 What happens if anybody get left behind?
4 What a boring town! There are not good clubs, nothing!
5 He was lonely because he had a few friends.
6 I've wasted two hours because the whole information you gave me was wrong.
7 When I got on the plane, I was told I could have some seat because there were so few passengers on that flight.
8 Her problem is that she has much homework to do so she has very little time for socialising.
9 I feel so embarrassed that all know my problem.
10 If I had lots of money I'd spend half it on a holiday and buy a house with the rest.

English Grammar in Use Supplementary Exercises

Quantifiers and pronouns

Units 86–91

159 Choose the correct alternative.

The place where I grew up

Last week I visited the remote country village where I grew up, in a region now popular with tourists. I remembered the two old-fashioned shops and a number of old houses in the hills. I realised very quickly that although in (1) <u>many / few</u> ways it appears unchanged, in reality hardly (2) <u>nothing / anything</u> is the same.

(3) <u>All / Every</u> the traditional houses are there, of course, and (4) <u>both / most</u> the shops. But (5) <u>none of the / none of</u> houses are owned by residents. All of (6) <u>they / them</u> belong to city people, who arrive (7) <u>every weekend / all the weekends</u> in their noisy new cars.

(8) <u>Neither of / Neither</u> the shops sells local goods these days; they have expensive foreign food chosen by (9) <u>somebody / anyone</u> in an office (10) <u>anywhere / somewhere</u> who has (11) <u>little / a little</u> knowledge of the region.

There are (12) <u>few / a few</u> new houses too, and they have (13) <u>no / none of</u> local character. You can see the same style (14) <u>anywhere / somewhere</u> in Europe. In fact (15) <u>the whole / whole</u> atmosphere of the village has changed so much that it is (16) <u>any / no</u> more interesting than any suburban street.

Relative clauses

Units 92–96

160 Can you answer the questions about the people in Box A? Use the information from Boxes B and C.

A

1 Who was Mary Seacole?
2 Who was Antonio Stradivari?
3 Who was Ibn Battuta?
4 Who was Marie Tussaud?
5 Who is Valentina Tereshkova?
6 Who was Katsushika Hokusai?
7 Who was Joseph Niépce?

B

Japanese man   Russian   Frenchman   Swiss woman   Italian   Moroccan   ~~Jamaican~~

C

He travelled through Africa and Asia.
He made wonderful violins.
~~She worked as a nurse and saved many lives.~~
He produced the first permanent photograph.
She opened a waxworks museum.
She was the first female astronaut.
He made the famous print *The Great Wave off Kanagawa*.

1 Mary Seacole was a Jamaican who worked as a nurse and saved many lives.
2
3
4
5
6
7

Relative clauses

Units 92–96

161

Complete the conversation with **who**, **that**, **whose** or **where**. If no word is necessary, leave the space empty (–).

Zoe and Pat are planning a party next Thursday.

ZOE: Well, who shall we ask to this party?
PAT: Oh, not too many. Just a few people (1) **–** we can be relaxed with.
ZOE: Yes, I agree. So, who, for example?
PAT: John and Jason, of course, and Carlo.
ZOE: Carlo? Who's he?
PAT: He's the Italian guy (2) **who** is staying with John.
ZOE: Oh, yeah. Is he the one (3) .... wallet got stolen when they were in London?
PAT: That's right. They caught the guy (4) .... took it, but he'd already spent all the money (5) .... Carlo had brought with him.
ZOE: Poor Carlo. Perhaps the party will cheer him up.
PAT: It might, if we ask the girl (6) .... he's been going out with.
ZOE: Who's that?
PAT: Celia's her name. She works in that cinema (7) .... they show all the new films.
ZOE: But will she be free on Thursday evening?
PAT: Yes, it's her evening off. That's the reason (8) .... I suggested Thursday.
ZOE: OK. Who else? What about Nicky and Cherry?
PAT: Are they the people (9) .... you went to France with?
ZOE: Yes. If they bring their boyfriends, that'll be ten of us. But have you got a room (10) .... is big enough? My landlady says we can't use her sitting-room because we made too much mess the last time (11) .... she let us have a party.
PAT: It's all right. Our house has got a basement (12) .... we store old furniture. If we clean it up, it'll be fine.
ZOE: Great. Let's go and have a look at it.

162

Complete the sentences with your own ideas. Use a relative pronoun.

1 I like meeting people _who have travelled widely_ .
2 I enjoy parties _which go on till dawn_ .
3 I avoid going to clubs ....
4 Most of my friends are people ....
5 I never wear clothes ....
6 My favourite films are those ....
7 I feel sorry for students ....
8 My best friend is someone ....
9 I'm going to buy a phone ....
10 I wish I had a job ....

Relative clauses

Units 92–96

163 Tick (✓) the sentence which matches the situation.

1 I have three umbrellas. I bought one of them in Paris. That one needs repairing.
   a The umbrella which I bought in Paris needs repairing. ✓
   b The umbrella, which I bought in Paris, needs repairing.

2 I have one colleague. He works extremely hard. He has few friends.
   a My colleague who works extremely hard is not very popular.
   b My colleague, who works extremely hard, is not very popular. ✓

3 I have several aunts. One works in New York. She's getting married.
   a My aunt who works in New York is getting married.
   b My aunt, who works in New York, is getting married.

4 Peter made some sandwiches. They have all been eaten. You made some too. Your sandwiches have not been eaten.
   a The sandwiches which Peter made have all been eaten.
   b The sandwiches, which Peter made, have all been eaten.

5 There was only one park in this town. Someone has built over it. We used to play in the park when we were children.
   a The local park where we played as children has been built over.
   b The local park, where we played as children, has been built over.

6 One of my French teachers helps me with my homework. The other one lives too far away.
   a The French teacher whose house is near mine helps me with my homework.
   b The French teacher, whose house is near mine, helps me with my homework.

7 You met one of my cousins last summer, the one from America. He's coming to stay again.
   a My American cousin who you met last summer is coming to stay again.
   b My American cousin, who you met last summer, is coming to stay again.

8 There were a lot of candidates in the presidential election. Three of them were women. The winner was one of them. She had campaigned for better housing conditions.
   a The woman who had campaigned for better housing conditions has been elected President.
   b The woman, who had campaigned for better housing conditions, has been elected President.

9 I received lots of flowers when I was ill, but only my boyfriend sent me roses. I put the roses in my favourite vase.
   a The roses which my boyfriend sent look beautiful in my favourite vase.
   b The roses, which my boyfriend sent, look beautiful in my favourite vase.

10 I took two cameras away with me. You lent me one of them. That's the one that got broken.
   a The camera which you lent me has been broken.
   b The camera, which you lent me, has been broken.

Adjectives and adverbs

Units 100–101

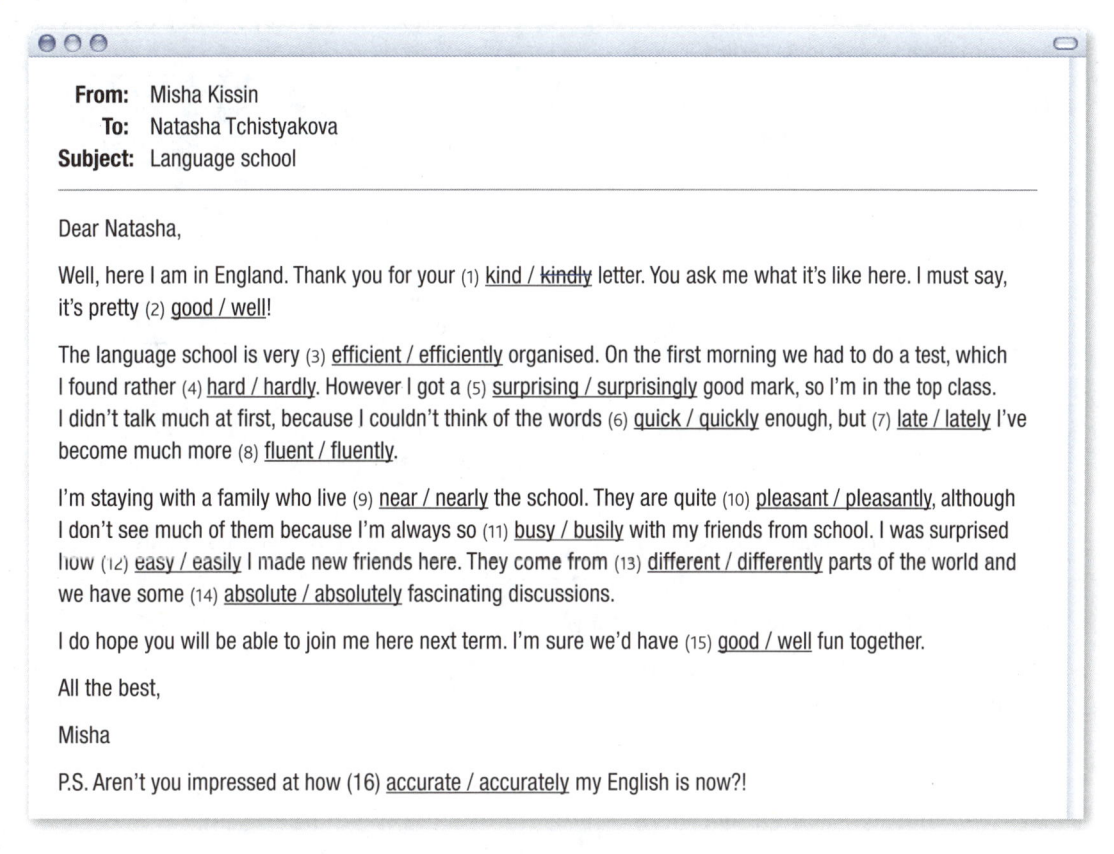

164 Choose the correct alternative.

From: Misha Kissin
To: Natasha Tchistyakova
Subject: Language school

Dear Natasha,

Well, here I am in England. Thank you for your (1) <u>kind / kindly</u> letter. You ask me what it's like here. I must say, it's pretty (2) <u>good / well</u>!

The language school is very (3) <u>efficient / efficiently</u> organised. On the first morning we had to do a test, which I found rather (4) <u>hard / hardly</u>. However I got a (5) <u>surprising / surprisingly</u> good mark, so I'm in the top class. I didn't talk much at first, because I couldn't think of the words (6) <u>quick / quickly</u> enough, but (7) <u>late / lately</u> I've become much more (8) <u>fluent / fluently</u>.

I'm staying with a family who live (9) <u>near / nearly</u> the school. They are quite (10) <u>pleasant / pleasantly</u>, although I don't see much of them because I'm always so (11) <u>busy / busily</u> with my friends from school. I was surprised how (12) <u>easy / easily</u> I made new friends here. They come from (13) <u>different / differently</u> parts of the world and we have some (14) <u>absolute / absolutely</u> fascinating discussions.

I do hope you will be able to join me here next term. I'm sure we'd have (15) <u>good / well</u> fun together.

All the best,

Misha

P.S. Aren't you impressed at how (16) <u>accurate / accurately</u> my English is now?!

165 There are mistakes in seven of these sentences. Correct the sentences where necessary. Write 'OK' if the sentence is already correct.

1 'Please get a move on!' <u>shouted Trevor impatient</u>. *shouted Trevor impatiently*
2 I believe she is a very lonely woman. *OK*
3 I didn't like his plan, which seemed unnecessary complicated to me.
4 I'm sure you could win the match if you tried hardly.
5 I have an awful headache, so could you please be quiet?
6 Soraya's only been in France a year, but she speaks perfectly French.
7 The reason Bruce gets so tired is that he has an exceptional demanding job.
8 My mother was ill last year, but she's good enough to go on holiday now.
9 David ran as fast as he could, but he still arrived late.
10 Jean always says she's short of money, but I happen to know she actually has a very good-paid job.

Comparatives and superlatives

Units 105–108

166 A class of students is studying environmental issues with their teacher. Look at the chart and complete their conversation.

TEACHER: On this bar chart, who recycled (1) _the highest_ percentage of glass in 2009?
FLORA: The Belgians did.
TEACHER: And who recycled (2) .... percentage?
WAYNE: The Poles.
TEACHER: Right. What about the Spanish? How well did they do?
JILL: They did (3) .... the Poles and Portuguese, but (4) .... the Czechs.
TEACHER: Did the Croatians recycle a (5) .... percentage of glass .... the Portuguese?
KEVIN: No, not quite. About five per cent (6) ....
TEACHER: What about the Norwegians?
BRONWEN: They recycled almost (7) .... percentage .... the Dutch.
TEACHER: Yes. That's over ten per cent (8) .... the Italians.
ALEX: But it's still seven per cent (9) .... the Belgians.
TEACHER: True. Now let's go on to talk about what we're going to do next.

Smashing figures?
% glass recycled by selected countries 2009

Belgium, Netherlands, Norway, Italy, Czech Republic, Spain, Portugal, Croatia, Poland (scale 40–100)

167 The class in the previous exercise took part in a paper recycling project. Look at the chart below and write sentences comparing the students' achievements.

FLORA 50 kilos, KEVIN 45 kilos, JILL 30 kilos, BRONWEN 30 kilos, ALEX 25 kilos, WAYNE 10 kilos

1 (Kevin / Flora / Jill)
  Kevin didn't collect as much paper as Flora, but he collected more than Jill.
2 (Alex / Bronwen / Jill) _Alex collected five kilos less than Bronwen or Jill._
3 (Flora) _Flora collected the most paper._
4 (Jill / Alex / Wayne) ....
5 (Bronwen / Jill) ....
6 (Wayne) ....
7 (Alex / Bronwen / Wayne) ....
8 (Jill / Flora / Alex) ....

Comparatives and superlatives — Units 105–108

168 Complete the conversations. Use the correct form of the word(s) given and any other words you need.

A JOE: Why have you bought a new car?
AMY: We needed one with a (1) *bigger* (big) boot, to take our sports gear.

B MARY: Which is (2) *the highest* (high / mountain) in Africa?
ANNE: I'm not sure. Kilimanjaro, perhaps?
MARY: Where's that? In Zambia?
ANNE: No, it's (3) *further north than* (far / north) that. Kenya I think.

C ANDY: Are you still having problems with your broadband connection?
JESS: Yes. I don't know what's wrong. I've tried contacting the server, but it's still (4) .... (fast) last week.

D ROSA: Which part of London has (5) .... (cheap) flats to rent, do you think?
ANA: I don't know. It's (6) .... (expensive) city in the country so they won't be cheap anywhere.
ROSA: I suppose the suburbs (7) .... (far) from the centre would be the place to look.
ANA: I'm not sure it works like that in London.

E FRED: How was your driving test?
JOSH: Oh, not so bad really. It was (8) .... (much / easy) I'd expected, in fact. And I passed!
FRED: Congratulations! That's (9) .... (good) news I've heard for ages!

F GAIL: Shall we go wind-surfing? It's lovely and sunny.
MICK: I'm not sure. The wind is good but I think you'll find it's (10) .... (not / warm) it looks when you get outside.

G EDDY: Let's go clubbing after we've eaten.
SEAN: Can't we go (11) .... (late)? I want to watch a film.
EDDY: No. The clubs shut (12) .... (early / here) they do at home.

H WILL: Come on! Can't you cycle (13) .... (fast)?
PETE: Sorry, I'm going (14) .... (fast) I can already.
WILL: Yeah, your bike's quite a bit (15) .... (old / mine), I guess.

I CHRIS: I hear you were having problems with your business last year. Is it (16) .... (good) this year?
JODIE: No. I'm afraid it's (17) .... (bad) if anything.
CHRIS: I suppose people just aren't spending (18) .... (much / money) they used to.

Word order

Units 109–110

169
Rewrite the sentences using the words in brackets.

1. We left early.
   (the meeting) _We left the meeting early._
2. We went to the cinema and we had a meal.
   (also) _____
3. My sister plays volleyball in summer.
   (in the park) _____
4. She's worked since she left school.
   (for that company) _____
5. If you order the trainers online, they'll be delivered by post.
   (now) (tomorrow) _____
6. He sends an email from his office every lunchtime.
   (his girlfriend) _____
7. When the flowers were delivered, was there a note?
   (with them) _____
8. We were late for work because of the traffic jam.
   (all) _____
9. I'm going to Zurich soon.
   (definitely) _____
10. The meal was lovely. My friends had asked the restaurant to make a birthday cake.
    (even) (for me) _____

170
Write three sentences about each of the three people in the left-hand column of the chart. Use the words in each row and add the adverbs at the top.

	occasionally	usually	hardly ever
Angela	arrives at work early	isn't in the office at lunchtime	has been off sick
John	is late in the morning	doesn't eat with his colleagues	answers emails promptly
Craig	has worked from home	drinks a lot of coffee	is in a bad temper

1. _Angela occasionally arrives at work early._
2. _John is occasionally late in the morning._
3. _____
4. _____
5. _____
6. _____
7. _____
8. _____
9. _____

Word order

Units 109–110

171 Rewrite each underlined sentence using the adverb in brackets.

Andy and Jane came home from shopping on Saturday to find their house had been burgled. A police officer has come to investigate the crime.

OFFICER: You say you're not sure how the thieves got in. Before I look round, can I ask you a few questions about the house?

ANDY: Of course.

OFFICER: (1) Do you lock the front door when you go out? (always)
Do you always lock the front door when you go out?

ANDY: (2) Yes, and I locked it yesterday. (definitely)
Yes, and I definitely locked it yesterday.

OFFICER: OK. What about the windows?

ANDY: (3) Well, the downstairs ones are locked. (always)

JANE: (4) We have a lock on the little one in the hall. (even)

OFFICER: And upstairs?

JANE: (5) Well, I think most of the windows were locked. (probably)

ANDY: (6) They were locked on Friday. (all)

JANE: Are you sure?

ANDY: (7) Yes, I knew we would be out all day, so I checked them all. (both)

OFFICER: And you didn't open any on Friday night?

ANDY: (8) No, I didn't. (certainly)

OFFICER: Well, I can't understand it. Let's look round. Perhaps I'll notice something you've missed.

172 Answer the questions using the words in brackets.

1 What does Tim have for breakfast? (has muesli with yogurt + usually)
   He *usually has muesli with yogurt*.

2 Why did James leave the party so early? (was getting bored + probably)
   He *was probably getting bored*.

3 Does Maggie go to a gym regularly? (doesn't belong to one + even)
   She ....

4 What does Saskia think of your new apartment? (has been there + never)
   She ....

5 Do you know where Maureen might be? (has a few days off at this time of year + often)
   She ....

6 How is Keith getting on with his assignment? (has finished it + almost)
   He ....

Prepositions of time

Units 119–122

173
Put in at, for, during, by, until or in.

The city of London was founded by the Romans (1) ...in... the year 43 AD.
(2) ...During... the next few years it quickly became the main trading centre in Britain.
(3) .... two hundred years after the Romans left, the city was almost forgotten. Its full importance did not return
(4) .... the eleventh century.
(5) .... the end of that century, the government of England was based in Westminster and the Tower of London had been started.
(6) .... the Middle Ages London continued to grow and (7) .... the time of Shakespeare, it had become a prosperous capital city with many fine buildings. Unfortunately, most of these buildings were made of wood and (8) .... 1666 they were almost all destroyed by a fire which lasted (9) .... several days. This was a great tragedy for the people living there
(10) .... that time, but it is true that many of the areas which are most attractive today were planned (11) .... the rebuilding which followed.

174
Answer the questions, beginning each answer with a preposition.

1 When's your birthday?
2 What year did you start school?
3 When do you usually have your main meal of the day?
4 What time of the year is it best to go on holiday?
5 When do you meet your friends?
6 When did you last receive a present from anyone?
7 How long have you been studying English?

Prepositions of time

Units 119–122

175

Complete the article with the prepositions from the box. If no word is necessary, leave the space empty (–).

at   by   during   for   in   on   until   while

THE WAY PEOPLE WORK

Erwin is a nurse who works the night shift. How does he manage?

'Well, I finish work (1) _at_ 6.30 am. Then I go home, have a shower and try to be in bed (2) _by_ half past eight. (3) .... the same time as I'm getting ready for bed, Joanne, my wife, and our four-year-old daughter, Elaine, are getting up. Joanne drops Elaine at nursery school, which she started (4) .... last year, on the way to her office.

I usually sleep (5) .... about three o'clock (6) .... the afternoon. I have to be at the school (7) .... 3.30 to collect Elaine. We come home and she plays or watches a cartoon (8) .... I prepare our meal.

When Joanne comes home from work, we eat. If we're lucky, we can relax (9) .... an hour before putting Elaine to bed. Then we do any chores that didn't get done earlier. I always allow plenty of time to get to the hospital because if I'm not there (10) .... time, another nurse will have to go on working (11) .... I arrive. I'm often very tired (12) .... the time I finish, but I don't really mind. There's a special atmosphere in the hospital (13) .... night. Of course, I have a free day (14) .... every week. And the hours suit us, (15) .... the moment anyway. I may want to work (16) .... the day when Elaine goes to a different school. Perhaps I'll be ready for a change (17) .... then.'

Prepositions of place

Units 123–126

176 Choose the correct alternative.

A JAY: Oh, look. Here's a photo taken in my classroom at primary school. Can you recognise me (1) **in** / on it?

ANNA: No, I don't think so. Unless that's you right (2) **in** / **at** the back.

JAY: No, that's not me. I'm the one standing (3) **in** / **at** the corner.

ANNA: In trouble as usual!

B PIA: I don't understand this.

LILY: What?

PIA: Well, I want to check something with the college, but it says (4) **in** / **on** this letter that I must give a reference number when I phone, and I can't find it.

LILY: It's in that little booklet, (5) **in** / **on** the first page.

PIA: Oops! So it is. Thanks.

C MEL: Did you see Yves (6) **in** / **at** the disco?

JAN: No, of course not. He returned (7) **to** / **in** France last week.

MEL: But I'm sure I saw him (8) **in** / **on** the bus yesterday. In fact, he waved to me when we arrived (9) **to** / **at** the bus station.

JAN: How strange. We'll have to investigate what he's up to!

177 Put in *in*, *at* or *on*.

Hi Hannu,

Many thanks for agreeing to stay in the flat and look after things while I'm away. Here are some notes about what's where, as promised.

<u>Key</u>

Anneka, who lives (1) __in__ the flat (2) _____ the ground floor has the key. If she's out, the landlord lives (3) _____ the building (4) _____ the end of the street. It's called Laurel Villa, and the landlord is Mr Amiri. They both know you'll be there while I'm away.

<u>Electricity and gas</u>

The electricity and gas main switches are (5) _____ the wall (6) _____ the back of the large cupboard (7) _____ the study.

<u>Water</u>

You can turn the water off by the large tap (8) _____ the corner of the bathroom. I hope you won't need to!

<u>Phone numbers</u>

I've made a list of all the useful phone numbers I can think of, for takeaway pizzas, taxi, etc. It's stuck (9) _____ the kitchen door.

I hope you have a good time.

Shiv

English Grammar in Use Supplementary Exercises

Prepositions (general)

Units 117, 127–128

178 Choose the correct alternative.

TROUBLE AT NORTON MINING

The workforce of Norton Mining has gone (1) <u>on</u> / <s>in</s> strike following a serious accident at the mine in Midsummer Valley in Virginia. The cause (2) <u>for / of</u> the accident is unclear, but miners are blaming management attitudes (3) <u>on / to</u> safety regulations. Damage (4) <u>of / to</u> equipment was frequently ignored and miners' demands (5) <u>for / of</u> safer working practices were rejected by the owner, John Norton. His relationship, (6) <u>with / to</u> the workforce was said to be very poor. Although there had recently been a rise (7) <u>of / in</u> the number of minor accidents, he claimed there was no need (8) <u>for / of</u> a change in working practices. Norton is away (9) <u>on / in</u> a business trip. A member of the office staff said she had spoken briefly to him (10) <u>by / on</u> the phone. The news of the accident had come (11) <u>like / as</u> a great shock to everyone in the office, she added. She was unable to say when he would be back. It is understood that the police would like to speak to Mr Norton in connection (12) <u>with / to</u> a number of his financial dealings.

179 Complete the answers. Use the words in brackets with one of the prepositions from the box and any other words you need.

| as | at | by | in | like | on |

1 What's this room? (store room)
  We use it _as a store room_ .
2 What would you like to do now? (shade)
  Let's sit _____ .
3 Why doesn't your friend eat bread? (special diet)
  His doctor has put him _____ .
4 Have you got enough money for your train ticket? (credit card)
  It's OK. I'll pay _____ .
5 Was the exhibition interesting? (recent college graduates)
  Yes. The works were all _____ .
6 Was your brother hurt when his car crashed? (20 km per hour)
  No. Luckily he was only travelling _____ .
7 Why are you writing so slowly? (capital letters)
  Because I have to put my address _____ .
8 Why is your hand so swollen? (wasp)
  I got stung _____ .
9 What colour is Danni's new bag? (the last one)
  It's navy blue, _____ .
10 What are you doing in the summer holidays? (motorcycle messenger)
  I've got a job _____ .

Adjective / verb + preposition

Units 130–136

180 Complete the sentences using the prepositions from the box and your own ideas.

| about | at | for | in | of | on |

1 I know someone who's brilliant _at playing the saxophone_ .
2 It's difficult to feel sorry ....
3 Athletes always feel proud ....
4 Most of my friends aren't interested ....
5 Many people are nervous ....
6 My mood depends ....
7 I enjoy laughing ....
8 Lots of children believe ....

181 Complete the email with the phrases from the box.

| ~~at remembering gossip~~   for giving up   in changing her opinion   of behaving   of Helen |
| of her behaviour   of making   on doing   on their advice   with her   with herself |

Hi Terri,
You asked me for news of Helen in your last email. Well, you know I'm completely hopeless (1) _at remembering gossip_ but basically the situation is this – Helen's parents haven't forgiven Helen (2) .... law and enrolling at art college. They thought she would rely (3) .... , but she says she's capable (4) .... her own decisions. Her parents have always been very tolerant (5) .... but they're really annoyed (6) .... because of this sudden change of plan.
When she told me, I could see she was really pleased (7) .... But her parents are quite upset, because they haven't succeeded (8) ....
Well, it's typical (9) .... She always insists (10) .... what she wants. I wouldn't dream (11) .... the way she does.
Anyway, that's how it is. How are you?

Love, Sue

182 Match the beginning of each sentence with the most suitable preposition. Then use your own ideas to complete the sentence.

1 The lorry collided   1 _b_   a of ....
2 The bus crashed   2 ...... b with _a car_ .
3 The square was full   3 ...... c from ....
4 The minibus belonged   4 ...... d on ....
5 They borrowed the car   5 ...... e into ....
6 They blamed the accident   6 ...... f to ....
7 The owner was upset   7 ...... g for ....
8 The driver apologised   8 ...... h about ....

English Grammar in Use Supplementary Exercises

Phrasal verbs

Units 137–145

183 Write a sentence for each picture. Use **going to** + a phrasal verb.

1. He 's going to throw them away.
2. She's _____.
3. She's _____.
4. He's _____.
5. She's _____.
6. He's _____.
7. He's _____.
8. She's _____.

Phrasal verbs

Units 137–145

184
Complete each sentence with a preposition.

1 I'm looking forward __to__ seeing my family again.
2 My uncle ran away _____ home when he was a teenager.
3 Have you ever fallen out _____ any of your neighbours?
4 How well does your brother get on _____ his classmates?
5 My dentist has told me that I must cut down _____ sweets.
6 We went up _____ a woman and asked her for directions.
7 My brother pointed his boss out _____ me as she came into the restaurant.
8 The new manager came up _____ several interesting suggestions.
9 I'll get back _____ you as soon as I've got any news.
10 My brother gets away _____ all sorts of things I wouldn't be allowed to do.

185
Complete each sentence with the correct form of **get** + one of the words from the box. Use one of the words twice.

| away | back | by | in | on | out |

1 The taxi stopped and a small boy __got out__, holding a bunch of flowers.
2 We haven't had a holiday yet this year. We've been too busy to _____ .
3 What time do you think you'll _____ here after the party?
4 The festival organisers employ security guards to prevent people _____ without tickets.
5 It's natural for parents to wonder how their children _____ when they're away at university.
6 Modern buses are designed to make it easy for passengers to _____ .
7 I don't earn much, but I try to _____ without borrowing.

186
Complete each sentence with the correct form of **take** + one of the words from the box. Use two of the words twice.

| away | down | in | off | up |

1 The woman __took off__ her jacket and began work.
2 I had to pay £100 to have my old car _____ .
3 Few of the criminals _____ by the policeman's attempt to disguise himself as a beggar.
4 The students were told to _____ the posters which they had hung from their windows.
5 My mother _____ yoga last year to keep herself fit.
6 I don't keep a lot of movies on my laptop because they _____ too much memory.
7 We were offered drinks soon after the plane _____ .

Phrasal verbs

Units 137–145

187

Complete each sentence with the correct form of **go** + one of the words from the box. Use two of the words twice.

> away   back   in   on   out

1 I know the house isn't empty because I saw a man ....*go in*.... about an hour ago.
2 I don't know what .... in that classroom, but they're making a lot of noise, whatever it is!
3 I'm sorry I interrupted you. What were you saying? Please ....
4 He was born in Scotland, but it's unlikely he .... to live there because he's lived in London for so long.
5 I'm sorry, you can't see the manager because he .... on business for a few days.
6 The green light on the front of the dishwasher .... Does that mean it's finished?
7 I .... for a walk but if you need anything you can text me.

188

Complete each sentence with the correct form of **put** + one of the words from the box. Use one of the words three times.

> back   down   off   on   out

1 One fire officer was slightly injured while ....*putting out*.... the fire in the hotel.
2 We have to allow plenty of time after swimming for the children to dry themselves and .... their clothes.
3 After cleaning, the paintings must .... in exactly the same places on the wall.
4 Is it OK to .... some music, or will it disturb you?
5 We'll have to .... the barbecue till another day if the weather doesn't improve.
6 Please .... that rucksack. It's much too heavy for you to carry.
7 It's cold in here. Shall I .... the central heating?

189

Complete each sentence with the correct form of **turn** + one of the words from the box. Use two of the words twice.

> down   off   on   out   up

1 I always ....*turn on*.... the television as soon as I get home.
2 We didn't expect good weather yesterday, but it .... quite warm.
3 I hadn't seen Fernando since we were students, then one day he .... and asked me to have lunch with him.
4 We weren't aware of it, but it .... that we had been staying at the same campsite as our friends.
5 Can you .... the volume? It's very quiet.
6 When the captain .... the engine, we could hear the birds in the trees by the river.
7 Go and ask your grandfather to .... his radio. It's far too loud.

English Grammar in Use Supplementary Exercises

Phrasal verbs

Units 137–145

190

Complete the announcement with the verbs from the box in the correct form and the words in brackets.

| cross out | fill in | hand back | ~~hand out~~ |
| hold up | leave out | rub out | tear up |

'Ladies and gentlemen, we will arrive at our next destination in three hours. At this port some passengers will need visas. In a few minutes members of the crew (1) _will hand out landing cards_ (landing cards). Please read the card carefully to check whether you need to (2) _____ (it). If you do not need the card, please (3) _____ (not / it), but (4) _____ (it) immediately to the crew member. When completing the card, be careful not to (5) _____ (any information). If you make a mistake, (6) _____ (it) neatly. Please do not try to (7) _____ (it) with an eraser. Failure to complete the form correctly will result in our whole group (8) _____ at the immigration office, so please read through what you have written. Thank you.'

191

Complete the newspaper article with the verbs from the box in the correct form and the words in brackets.

| break down | bring up | fall out with | find out | keep away |
| let down | put up with | run away from | show off | ~~split up~~ |

STAR ADMITS HEARTBREAK

Friends of TV celebrity couple Rosie and Jeff have confirmed that they (1) _are splitting up_. They say Rosie (2) _____ that Jeff is seeing another woman. 'The relationship (3) _____ ,' revealed a tearful Rosie. 'I'm not prepared to (4) _____ him any longer,' she added. 'He (5) _____ in nightclubs and he (6) _____ (me) in front of my friends.' Rosie plans to (7) _____ (their daughter Mimi) on her own, but she (8) _____ (not / her) from Jeff. 'Just because we (9) _____ each other, it doesn't mean he can (10) _____ his responsibilities to Mimi,' she said. Rosie hopes to find love again but, for now, she wants to spend time with her family.

116   English Grammar in Use Supplementary Exercises

Phrasal verbs

Units 137–145

192

Complete the news item with the verbs from the box in the correct form and the words in brackets.

| bring up | close down | do up | hold up | pay back | rip off | ~~set up~~ |

LAST CALL FOR HITTRONICS.COM

Talks are being held with suppliers of Hittronics.com, the high street company which (1) __was set up__ by Antonia Highbridge only three years ago with £20m of her family's money. Her billionaire parents say she must (2) _____ (them) this month or her business will have to (3) _____. Customers have claimed that Highbridge (4) _____ (them) with poor goods and inefficient service. Highbridge stated yesterday that her problems began because her business development plans (5) _____ by the family's attitude. 'Our stores look dated and I asked for extra capital so that we can (6) _____ (them). But every time I (7) _____ (the subject), the family said I had to wait.'

193

Complete the newspaper article with the verbs from the box in the correct form.

| blow up | ~~break down~~ | drive away | drop off | give up | go off | go on | ride off |

NOISES IN THE NIGHT

Residents of Victoria Street in Thornton were disturbed last night by an unusual accident. At eleven o'clock a car (1) __broke down__ near the end of the street and the driver left his vehicle there while he (2) _____ with his journey by taxi. An hour later, the car's alarm (3) _____ when it was hit by a stolen van. The engine of the van (4) _____, so the thief tried to (5) _____ in the car. But he (6) _____ when the car wouldn't start and stole a bicycle instead. 'I (7) _____ to sleep at about midnight,' said Michael Patel who lives at 11 Victoria Street, 'then I was woken by a terrible ringing and a loud bang. When I looked out of my window, I saw a man (8) _____ on my bicycle!'

Phrasal verbs

Units 137–145

194 Rewrite the sentences replacing the underlined verbs with the verbs from the box in the correct form.

| carry on | cut down | find out | leave out | ~~look back on~~ |
| plug in | put off | put up with | turn down | work out |

1 I'm sure we'll all remember this holiday with great pleasure.
   I'm sure we'll all look back on this holiday with great pleasure.

2 He calculated that it would cost $100,000 to do a degree in the States.

3 This lead should be connected to the back of your computer.

4 You have omitted several important facts in your report.

5 We can't continue if you won't co-operate.

6 He was offered a new job, but he refused it because he didn't want to move house.

7 We moved house because we couldn't bear the noise from the motorway any longer.

8 He had to leave when his boss discovered what he had been doing.

9 Potential customers were discouraged by the difficulty of parking near the restaurant.

10 The company has succeeded in reducing the packaging it uses by twenty-five per cent.

195 Rewrite this email using the verbs from the box in the correct form.

| come up with | drop out of | get away with | ~~get out of~~ | let down | put up with |

Hi Mac, how are you? I'm fed up. I have to work hard but my cousin
Ruth is so spoilt. She always manages to avoid anything difficult. *get out of*
She used to invent all kinds of excuses when she was younger.
Now she's left college without finishing her course. Her father
says he won't tolerate her behaviour any longer, but I bet Ruth
won't be punished for it, as usual.
If I disappointed my parents like she does, I'd be in real trouble!
See you soon, Ali

Phrasal verbs

Units 137–145

196
Complete the sentences with suitable verbs in the correct form.

1 If you're offered the job, surely you won't ....*turn*.... it down?
2 Never .... off until tomorrow what you can do today.
3 The departure of the plane .... up by poor weather.
4 I .... out the mistake and wrote the correct word.
5 My cousins .... up by their grandmother as their parents worked abroad.
6 The festival blamed the mistake on the ticket agency, who .... them down.
7 I'm no good at .... up stories, but I'll read you one if you like.
8 A cat got into the museum and .... off the burglar alarm.

197
Complete each answer with a suitable phrasal verb + a pronoun where necessary.

1 NINA: What shall I do about this form on the website?
  JOHN: Just ....*fill it in*.... online and click 'send'.

2 FRED: Is Sonia a fast runner?
  SUE: Oh, yes. Nobody else on the team can ....

3 ALAN: Why didn't you buy a new computer game?
  DAVE: The shop has .... the latest ones.

4 MAY: Did you believe Nicola's story?
  EVAN: No, I knew she must have ....

5 GREG: Do we need to make a sauce for dinner this evening?
  BILL: Yes, so you'd better ....

6 CILLA: What are the girls doing in the garden with the tent?
  ALEC: They want to .... before they go away, to check that it's OK.

7 LEE: Were you disappointed that Graham didn't keep his promise?
  RUTH: Yes, we all felt he'd .... rather badly.

8 IAN: Did Francesca play with her cousins when they came to stay?
  JIM: Oh, yes. She .... very well.

198
Complete the sentences with your own ideas. Use **on** or **off**.

1 I turned ....*off the television and went out*.... .
2 The children set ....
3 The lazy student put ....
4 I tried ....
5 Our plane took ....
6 The girl switched ....
7 The boys carried ....
8 The teenagers showed ....

Phrasal verbs

Units 137–145

199 Complete the sentences with your own ideas. Use **up** or **down**.

1 The young businessman set _up his own company making computer games_.
2 My boyfriend turned ....
3 The old lady put ....
4 My grandfather took ....
5 The workmen knocked ....
6 The gangsters beat ....
7 The young couple were saving ....
8 The business closed ....

200 Complete the sentences with your own ideas. Use **in** or **out**.

1 We often eat _out on Saturday evenings_.
2 The prisoner climbed ....
3 The new student joined ....
4 Air travellers must check ....
5 The picture has been cut ....
6 The schoolboy let ....
7 My secretary will sort ....
8 The investigation was carried ....

Solution to Exercise 143

9.05 Lucy left the study.
Trevor phoned Gerald.
9.15 Lucy saw Gerald on the phone.
Delia and Doctor Emerson heard Trevor shouting at Gerald, on the phone. When he was checking the accounts, he discovered that Gerald had been stealing from the business.
9.25 Doctor Emerson left, banging the front door.
9.30 Gerald entered the house and killed Trevor after a short argument.
9.40 Gerald left the house and met Lucy on her way home.

Key

1
2 is singing
3 are playing
4 are holding
5 are offering
6 is organising

2
2 I'm meeting
3 Is this music disturbing
4 I'm enjoying
5 Is anyone using
6 We're having
7 are those people shouting
8 They're demonstrating
9 Are you applying
10 I'm thinking
11 Is Jane leaving
12 she's flying
13 Are you coming
14 I'm working

3
2 's standing / is standing
3 aren't looking / are not looking
4 's wearing / is wearing
5 isn't wearing / is not wearing
6 's watching / is watching
7 's shining / is shining
8 is hanging
9 's lying / is lying

4
Students' own answers. See Exercise 3 for model answer.

5
2 passes
3 takes
4 lasts
5 don't sing
6 keep
7 doesn't happen
8 enjoy
9 don't remember
10 occurs
11 falls
12 looks
13 comes

6
2 does the bank shut
3 Does your flat have
4 do you see
5 don't you drive
6 does your sister keep
7 Don't you want
8 do you work
9 do you spend
10 Doesn't the souvenir shop sell

7
2 doesn't start
3 I'm making
4 I'm staying
5 own
6 we drive
7 I'm making
8 I think
9 I understand
10 I help
11 he's working
12 he needs
13 I'm learning
14 do
15 Are you coming
16 I'm spending
17 They want
18 it gets
19 you decide
20 you're doing

8
Example answers:
4 My father is working in Poland this year.
5 My wife goes to the gym every week.
6 Several of my colleagues are learning English at the moment.
7 Our next-door neighbour is building a garage this year.
8 Our children go to bed late at weekends.
9 I'm working hard this term.
10 My best friend is waiting for me right now.

9
2 don't know
3 are trying
4 believe
5 have
6 helps
7 are disappearing
8 aren't doing
9 consist
10 melt
11 agree
12 are already rising

10
2 Both
3 Are you enjoying your meal?
4 I'm thinking of selling my car.
5 Both
6 I don't believe his story.
7 The students seem tired today.
8 He weighs 80 kilos.
9 How often do you play tennis?
10 My brother is looking for a new job.

11
2 had
3 visited
4 discussed
5 wasn't
6 drove
7 met
8 looked
9 went
10 invited
11 weren't
12 caught

12
See Exercise 11 for model answer.

13
3 While he was walking in the mountains, Harry saw a bear.
4 The students were playing a game when the professor arrived.
5 Felix phoned the fire brigade when the cooker caught fire.
6 When the starter fired her pistol, the race began.
7 I was walking home when it started to snow.
8 Andy was having lunch in a cafe when Juno phoned.

14
2 was lying
3 didn't wash
4 was eating
5 noticed
6 tasted
7 became
8 was working
9 was tidying
10 saw
11 didn't have

English Grammar in Use Supplementary Exercises

Key

12 was growing
13 was preparing
14 realised
15 decided
16 didn't melt
17 was walking
18 felt
19 was melting
20 led

15
2 met
3 was travelling
4 were shopping
5 went
6 was looking
7 came
8 started
9 called
10 thought
11 was trying
12 was
13 wasn't stealing
14 belonged
15 didn't mind
16 asked
17 got married
18 didn't know

16
2 gave
3 was passing
4 heard
5 banged
6 invited
7 was organising
8 didn't accept
9 was preparing
10 passed
11 went
12 met
13 was studying
14 didn't have
15 worked
16 were serving
17 announced
18 persuaded
19 were
20 was
21 earned
22 decided

17
Example answers:
2 I was walking home when it started to rain. I decided to catch the bus.
3 Everyone was dancing when the lights went out. We tried to phone the electricity company.
4 When we came out of the cinema, the sun was shining. We went to the park for an ice cream.

18
2 I'm looking
3 they're building
4 they look
5 I think
6 do you want
7 are getting
8 did you decide
9 we were staying
10 we're trying
11 we aren't looking
12 We don't have
13 We want
14 did
15 lent
16 we managed
17 we choose
18 gave
19 I was looking
20 I bumped

19
2 didn't understand
3 tastes
4 believed
5 doesn't belong
6 are you wearing
7 was jogging
8 stole
9 Do you see
10 prefer

20
3 because the engineer **didn't call** for help
4 OK
5 **Is** her health **improving**?
6 I completely **agree** with you.
7 What **did you do** after you left school?
8 OK
9 why you **believed** all those stories
10 Martin **was looking** forward to
11 OK
12 Where **do you keep** the paper towels?

21
Example answers:
2 'm beginning/am beginning
3 hurts
4 walk
5 met
6 were having
7 walked
8 was walking
9 began
10 'm being/am being
11 managed
12 were looking
13 want
14 is beginning
15 get

22
2 do you clean
3 did you pass
4 Are you watching
5 did you go
6 Do you think
7 were you doing
8 does the post office open

23
2 have already done
3 I've only been
4 I haven't slept
5 I've taken
6 's shown/has shown
7 I've eaten
8 I've ridden
9 I've travelled
10 I haven't spent
11 's paid/has paid
12 I've had

24
2 c 3 b 4 a 5 b 6 c

25
2 've been coming / have been coming *or* 've come / have come
3 've been driving / have been driving

Key

4 've never had / have never had
5 've always been / have always been
6 've had / have had
7 've done / have done
8 've been doing / have been doing
9 've looked / have looked *or* 've been looking / have been looking
10 haven't found

26
2 *Both*
3 *Both*
4 I've known her for two years.
5 *Both*
6 *Both*
7 They've seen this movie before.
8 *Both*
9 We've realised where we are now.
10 It's belonged to us for many years.
11 *Both*
12 You've broken my phone!

27
2 I've forgotten
3 Have you had
4 Have you been playing about
5 Have you been studying
6 You've never asked
7 he's failed … He hasn't been working
8 She's been repairing
9 They've been swimming
10 I've been doing
11 I've lost
12 You've been grumbling
13 she's been spending … She's bought … she's moved … She's been giving

28
Example answers:
2 've/have dropped my old one *or* 've/have broken my old one
3 've/have been cooking
4 've/have been going to dancing school *or* 've/have been having lessons
5 's/has gone to Australia
6 've/have been to the hairdresser *or* 've/have had my hair done
7 've/have been chopping onions
8 've/have sold my car

29
2 haven't/have not worn a long dress
3 hasn't/has not seen his brother
4 gone
5 since you learnt
6 been scuba diving since
7 since you topped up
8 been looking for
9 haven't/'ve never/have not been
10 hasn't had

30
Example answers:
3 I've been working from home for several years.
4 I've had a cold since yesterday.
5 When I was a child, I went swimming every day.
6 I started this exercise ten minutes ago.
7 It's three weeks since I saw my girlfriend.
8 For the past three weeks she's been working abroad.
9 I left school in 2010.
10 I've been feeling cold since I came into this room.
11 Last December I passed my driving test.
12 I haven't felt well since I got up this morning.

31
2 I've been revising
3 who's been looking
4 He's offered
5 I've been looking
6 He's designed
7 he doesn't have
8 he needs
9 He's been looking
10 I've been telling
11 He looks
12 He's coming
13 Are you using
14 I come
15 I've been checking
16 do you enjoy
17 I own

32
2 don't want … 've had / have had
3 's been suffering / has been suffering … 's seen / has seen
4 don't know … hasn't spoken
5 are you staring … haven't seen
6 'm staying / am staying … haven't been … 's lived / has lived *or* 's been living / has been living
7 Have you been waiting
8 've been watching / have been watching

33
Example answers:
2 've/have been
3 've/have decided
4 're/are enjoying
5 've/have seen
6 walked
7 took
8 haven't bought
9 've/have visited
10 hasn't been
11 say
12 snows
13 've/have been
14 think

34
2 we've been *or* we have been
3 what's causing *or* what is causing
4 we've been practising / we have been practising *or* we've practised / we have practised
5 that's really made *or* that really makes
6 we always win
7 we don't practise
8 We're playing / We are playing *or* We play
9 everyone agrees
10 we haven't practised
11 you have
12 who's been playing / who has been playing
13 he usually scores

English Grammar in Use Supplementary Exercises

Key

14 he's been arriving / he has been arriving
15 have begun / are beginning
16 he refuses
17 I say
18 he doesn't listen
19 I don't like
20 I hope

35
2 I **have lived** here ever since *or* I **have been living** here ever since
3 I left school **three years ago** and
4 since then I **have had** several jobs
5 For the past six months I **have been working** for Go-Places Agency.
6 The manager **has said** that he is willing
7 I **have also been learning** Spanish

36
Example answer:
Dear Ms Sparks,
I would like to apply for the job in a souvenir shop which I have seen advertised on the student jobsearch website. I am seventeen years old. My first language is Italian, but I also speak quite good German and English. I have not yet left school, but I have some experience in working in a shop as I sometimes help my uncle who runs a small supermarket. I attach the address and phone number of my teacher, Mr Pallini, who has said that he is willing to give me a reference. I hope you will consider my application.
Yours sincerely,

37
2 d 3 b 4 f 5 a
6 g 7 e

38
2 did you study … you qualified
3 did you first meet
4 you've cooked
5 We wanted … we didn't have
6 has happened … We've been texting you … he still hasn't replied
7 We posted … you haven't received
8 I've been working … I never realised

39
2 went
3 's been / has been
4 trained
5 has Neil had
6 Has Tina phoned
7 've broken / have broken
8 told
9 've forgotten / have forgotten
10 earned
11 Did Mark give
12 's offered / has offered

40
2 has seen
3 took
4 spent
5 required
6 has become
7 has enabled
8 have transformed
9 have improved
10 has replaced
11 knew
12 have learnt
13 haven't done / have not done
14 has brought
15 has solved

41
Example answers:
2 have you been
3 did you do *or* was the
4 did you need
5 did you want
6 have you been to *or* have you visited
7 did you stay
8 Have you brought *or* Did you bring
9 did you do
10 Did you do *or* Did you paint
11 did you become

42
Example answers:
2 Yesterday I studied English.
3 In the past six months I've done the washing up every day.
4 Since my last birthday I've played golf twice a week.
5 I haven't driven a car recently.
6 Last year I got married.
7 Six months ago I passed an important exam.
8 I haven't ridden a bike since I was a child.
9 I ate noodles yesterday evening.
10 This week I've texted my best friend a hundred times.

43
2 had prepared
3 arrived
4 discovered
5 had reserved
6 didn't have
7 had given
8 had also misunderstood
9 wanted
10 suspected
11 had lost

44
2 the match **had ended**
3 he **hadn't brought**
4 Gary **had** his laptop
5 I **found**
6 the lab **had mixed up**
7 because I **hadn't seen** him
8 so we **decided**

45
Example answers:
2 'd/had forgotten my birthday
3 'd/had gone out
4 he'd/had an accident
5 'd/had been eating sweets
6 'd/had been texting a friend
7 'd/had broken her leg
8 'd/had been stealing money *or* 'd/had stolen money

46
2 We'd arranged
3 didn't you come
4 I was
5 I'd been waiting
6 Didn't you get
7 I sent
8 I was walking

124   English Grammar in Use Supplementary Exercises

Key

9 I noticed
10 they'd changed
11 I texted
12 I didn't get
13 I was waiting
14 I was worrying
15 what had happened
16 I saw
17 You were laughing
18 I realised
19 you'd been sitting
20 I lost
21 My sister saw
22 She was singing

47
Example answers:
2 I didn't use to like olives.
3 I used to enjoy meeting new people.
4 My sister didn't use to be interested in visiting art galleries.
5 I used to play football more often.
6 My brother used to have long hair.
7 My uncle didn't use to live near us.
8 My husband used to work in Beijing.
9 I used to teach at the university.
10 We didn't use to cycle.

48
2 found
3 used to wear
4 Did people really use to think
5 admitted
6 often used to fall
7 were
8 was planning
9 was wearing

49
3 My girlfriend used to have a favourite handbag which she had bought with her first wages.
4 No change
5 Before the new shopping centre was built, there used to be a football stadium here.
6 Jasper complained that the street didn't use to be full of litter until the fast food restaurant opened.
7 During our cruise I took several photos of the seabirds which used to follow the ship.
8 No change
9 The music in this club used to be very boring before they installed a new sound system.
10 I used to spend a lot of time helping with the housework when I was a kid, but my sister didn't use to help at all.
11 No change

50
Example answers:
3 I used to watch television every day after school.
4 I used to go to the cinema every weekend, but I don't have time now.
5 I didn't use to have so much homework at my last school.
6 I didn't use to eat in restaurants, but now I go several times a week.
7 I used to listen to music while I was working, but my new boss doesn't allow it.
8 I used to see my grandparents every week when I was younger.

51
Example answers:
2 didn't use to be
3 had
4 used to stay
5 was booking/buying
6 fell
7 learnt/learned … was working
8 used to live

52
2 you were
3 Do you know
4 I used to eat
5 I was doing
6 did you hear
7 I phoned
8 She was checking
9 I rang
10 she told
11 Had you been expecting
12 Have you texted
13 He's been waiting

53
2 did you visit … you were
3 haven't topped up … do you think
4 realised … had driven
5 seems … she's been taking … advised
6 set … was frying … 's/has been sorting
7 spent … had missed … were
8 've/have always wanted … have …'ve/have decided
9 arrived … had got … was
10 's/is having … wants

54
2 that only lasts
3 I'll get
4 does your evening class finish
5 Shall I come
6 I'm meeting
7 will you talk
8 he won't let
9 I'm playing
10 I'll try
11 he'll agree

55
2 're working / are working
3 will let
4 includes
5 'll be / will be
6 'm seeing / am seeing
7 'll do / will do

56
2 I'll collect / I shall collect
3 I'll have to
4 there will probably be
5 a local student is coming
6 We'll be able to
7 the conference doesn't start
8 they're emailing
9 I'll read
10 I'll be

57
Example answers:
3 Next summer I'm visiting my cousins in Sardinia.
4 When I finish this exercise, I

English Grammar in Use Supplementary Exercises

Key

shall be happy.
5 Tomorrow evening I expect I'll eat out with my friends.
6 At the end of my course I'll probably speak quite good English.
7 My next class begins at six o'clock.
8 Next week we're having a class party.
9 My course finishes on 30th May.

58
2 I won't be late.
3 I'll deliver the goods on Friday.
4 Shall we go to the swimming pool?
5 Will you stop fighting!
6 The door won't open.
7 Shall I phone for an ambulance? *or* I'll phone for an ambulance.
8 I won't pay for the goods until I've checked that they aren't damaged.

59
2 It's going to rain very soon.
3 He's going to be in trouble.
4 Who's going to help me tidy up?
5 They're going to buy a tent.
6 I'm not going to come to this club again.
7 I'm going to walk to work from now on.
8 I'm going to have another coffee.
9 How are we going to get home?
10 I'm going to buy petrol tonight.
11 They're going to travel to Prague by train.
12 How are we going to contact her?

60
2 won't do
3 I'm going to go
4 Will you hold
5 they're going to raise
6 won't start
7 I'm going to start
8 I'll cook

9 they won't change
10 Shall we eat
11 He's going to buy
12 I'm going to go

61
3 people will come
4 I'll phone
5 Shall I phone
6 I'm going to see
7 Will he help
8 We're going to advertise
9 The bank will lend
10 We'll do
11 I'll help

62
Example answers:
3 will I
4 I'll send
5 I'm going to visit
6 I'll give
7 Will
8 I'll go
9 Will you wash
10 I won't

63
2 I'm meeting my grandmother (at the airport).
3 I'll pay you back at the weekend.
4 Why won't you tell me (the address)?
5 I'm not going to fail again.
6 Will you please turn the volume down?
7 I'm going to be in a film!
8 Which countries are you going to visit?

64
3 I'm meeting
4 I'll make
5 finishes
6 Shall I bring
7 I'm going to try
8 you get
9 I probably won't have
10 my course starts
11 I arrive
12 I'm spending
13 you'll be doing
14 I'll be getting
15 I'll Skype

65
2 could go
3 was able to get
4 haven't been able to
5 could be
6 couldn't
7 could have cooked

66
2 b   7 a and b
3 a and b   8 a
4 b   9 a
5 a   10 b
6 b

67
3 They might have had a row.
4 She might have dropped something.
5 It might be under the bed.
6 They might be planning a surprise.
7 He might have had some bad news.
8 She might be working at home.
9 She might have had something better to do.
You can use may *instead of* might *in all these sentences.*

68
Example answers:
3 you might get lost
4 you might miss your flight
5 you might damage your health
6 you might fail it
7 it might break down
8 you might be late on the first day
9 you might lose your job
10 he might get upset

69
2 c 3 f 4 e 5 a
6 b 7 h 8 i 9 g

70
2 could have fallen
3 may have found
4 may not have done
5 couldn't have left
6 could be coming
7 may be visiting
8 may be seeing

Key

71
2 must have been
3 can't be
4 can't be using
5 may be having
6 can't have enjoyed
7 may be delivering
8 can't have been concentrating
9 must be

72
Example answers:
3 might be
4 can't be
5 might be in
6 must have been
7 might not have seen
8 can't have told
9 might be something you

73
2 d 3 a 4 f 5 e
6 g 7 b

74
2 should have told
3 ought to
4 don't have to
5 needn't have bothered
6 must have sent
7 should be
8 must have forgotten

75
2 same
3 a = There's no reason for us to spend a long time in the museum if it's not interesting; b = I don't want to waste time in the museum if it's not interesting
4 b = I believe you opened the package (but this does not mean that I think you were wrong to do that)
5 same
6 a = We had too many sandwiches (for a past occasion); b = I'm about to make some sandwiches, but I'm not going to make as many as I originally planned to make (for a future occasion)
7 a = My father must not find out what I've done;
b = I've done something and I believe my father now knows about it
8 a = I think moving house now would be a mistake; b = I think moving now is unnecessary (but does not mean it would be a mistake)
9 same
10 a = We're about to leave and I suggest checking the timetable first (future); b = We left home but we didn't check the timetable before leaving and now we realise this was a mistake (past)

76
2 needn't   6 mustn't
3 Shouldn't   7 should
4 shouldn't   8 needn't
5 needn't

77
2 needn't   5 shouldn't
3 must   6 should
4 should   7 mustn't

78
1 shouldn't   4 shouldn't
2 needn't   5 should
3 should   6 must

79
Example answers:
2 ought not to spend the weekend at a music festival
3 ought to have visited me
4 ought not to have used it
5 ought not to have said it had unlimited texts
6 ought to have booked seats

80
2 a and b   7 a and b
3 a   8 a
4 a and b   9 a
5 a and b   10 a and b
6 a

81
2 'd better / had better / should
3 have to
4 have to / should
5 should
6 don't have to
7 'd better / had better / should
8 have to
9 'd better not / had better not / shouldn't
10 have to
11 should
12 'd better / had better / should

82
2 should check that all the windows are shut whenever you go out
3 shouldn't borrow money from people you hardly know
4 'd better / should keep the door shut in case someone sees us
5 have to train regularly if you want to succeed in athletics
6 'd better not / shouldn't take your phone to the beach. It might get stolen
7 'd better / should change your shirt before the guests arrive
8 don't have to pay extra for delivery

83
2 a, b, c   5 a, b
3 a, b   6 a, b, c
4 b, c

84
2 he recommended (that) I (should) **book** online / he recommended **booking** online
3 OK
4 I (should) **contact** my office
5 OK (*wouldn't* would also be possible)
6 Should my phone **be** off
7 OK
8 Why didn't you demand (that) the club (should) **refund** your subscription / (that) the club **refunded** your subscription?

85
2 the figures should disappear
3 I check
4 we discuss
5 I shouldn't bother
6 I find
7 anyone should call
8 we wait
9 we hire
10 he should be

English Grammar in Use Supplementary Exercises

Key

86
Example answers:
2 set my alarm clock
3 change them
4 go another day
5 make promises they can't keep
6 travel by train
7 be very difficult
8 forgotten I'm waiting for him
9 take regular exercise
10 go to work by bus
11 been very slow
12 find a seat
13 ride a horse … drive a car
14 show her the way

87
Example answers:
1 play games on your phone during lessons
2 keep a note of new vocabulary
3 arrive late for meetings
4 pay your fees at the beginning of term
5 wear smart clothes
6 work on Sundays

88
2 he doesn't arrive
3 won't refund
4 you reach
5 will you cut
6 Would you work
7 didn't complain
8 Wouldn't my friends be

89
2 will it cost
3 would it help
4 would you buy
5 will you do
6 would you say

90
2 he didn't like
3 You'll see
4 Wouldn't your boyfriend be
5 I don't revise
6 would you look for
7 she wasn't/weren't
8 would you feel
9 you could

91
2 If you could find/found a job using your languages, would you take it?
3 If it was/were in South America, I'd/would certainly consider it carefully.
4 That'd/would be a great way to travel if you could speak/spoke the right languages.
5 I'd/would only consider a job like that if I was/were sure the travel company was a good one.
6 If the tourists didn't like their hotels and so on, I'd/would have a terrible time.
7 You'd/would/could be handling complaints every day if they weren't happy.
8 But if I decide to apply for a job like that, will you help me with my application? / But if I decided to apply for a job like that, would you help me with my application?
9 you'll/will succeed, if you do.

92
Example answers:
2 What would you do if you won a lottery prize?
3 What would you do if you saw someone being mugged?
4 What would you do if your house was on fire?
5 What would you do if you were having a problem with grammar?
6 How would your brother react if you crashed his car?
7 What would happen if your teacher stepped on a banana skin?
8 What would happen if you overslept?
9 What would you and your friends do if you didn't have to earn money?
10 What would happen to car manufacturers if we all rode bikes?
11 What would happen if all the politicians retired?
12 What would you do if you felt ill when you woke up?

93
Your answers should have the same structures as those in Exercise 92.

94
2 f 3 a 4 b 5 g
6 c 7 d

95
Example answers:
2 'd/would do … had … were/was … 'd/would want
3 'd/had known … wouldn't have asked
4 wouldn't have hurt … hadn't been reading
5 love … were/was … lost … would you do

96
Example answers:
2 If she'd had a holiday last year, she wouldn't have got terribly tired and stressed.
3 If her manager hadn't contracted her to record a new album after the tour, he wouldn't have panicked.
4 If the tour hadn't been such a huge success, she wouldn't have been able to postpone the recording for two months.
5 If her manager hadn't sent her to a luxury spa hotel for a complete rest, she wouldn't have met Hossein.
6 If Hossein hadn't been recovering from a bad skiing accident, he would have been doing research in California.
7 If they hadn't been the only guests on their own, they wouldn't have started talking.
8 If he'd known who she was, he would have treated her like a star.
9 If her manager hadn't panicked, she wouldn't have met her fiance.

Key

97
Example answers:
3 If I'd come home earlier, I wouldn't be so tired.
4 If I'd had some breakfast, I'd be able to concentrate.
5 If I'd remembered to book seats last week, we could go to the concert. / could have gone to the concert.
6 If I hadn't missed the bus, I wouldn't have been fired.
7 If I hadn't broken my leg (when I went skiing), I could go to the wedding. / could have gone to the wedding.
8 If we'd stopped to buy some petrol, we wouldn't have run out.

98
Example answers:
2 wasn't/weren't so mean
3 couldn't have watched the match
4 hadn't been reading in the car
5 would be more popular
6 apologise
7 pressed this button
8 hadn't been unlucky
9 'd/had borrowed their bikes
10 would have made a lot of money

99
4 had … could take a lot of exercise
5 didn't leave their bikes unlocked … wouldn't be so easy for thieves
6 had realised how dangerous smoking was … wouldn't have serious health problems
7 would have risen … hadn't forgotten to add yeast / had added yeast
8 don't protect wildlife now … won't be any left
9 realised how much toys cost … 'd/would understand

100
2 I wish I had a car.
3 I wish I worked in an office.
4 I wish I lived with my son.
5 I wish I could swim.
6 I wish I didn't live in a city.
7 I wish I were/was a helicopter pilot.
8 I wish I didn't have short hair.

101
Example answers:
Martin:
I wish he'd wash his coffee mug.
I wish he wouldn't leave his shoes lying around the room.
I wish he wouldn't drop his clothes on my chair.
I wish he wouldn't come in late.
I wish he'd remember I go to sleep early.
I wish he wouldn't lie in bed playing computer games.
Bernie:
I wish he wouldn't work so hard.
I wish he didn't get so angry when I make a phone call.
I wish he wouldn't interfere with my possessions.
I wish he wouldn't move my clothes around so I can't find them.
I wish he wouldn't throw my shoes on my bed.
I wish he'd play computer games with me sometimes.
I wish he wouldn't wake me up when he goes for a run.
I wish he were/was fun to share a room with.

102
2 wish I had
3 wish I had learned/learnt
4 wish I'd realised
5 wishes they hadn't moved
6 wish I knew
7 wish they'd never started

103
2 is/was played by Johnny Depp
3 were built by the Ancient Egyptians
4 was invented by Guglielmo Marconi
5 was painted by Pablo Picasso
6 was developed by Sir Tim Berners-Lee
7 was designed by Gustave Eiffel
8 was discovered by Crick and Watson
9 was invented by the Chinese
10 was discovered by Marie Curie

104
3 The puncture has been mended.
4 The concert has been cancelled.
5 Jane Jones has been elected.
6 The rabbit has disappeared.
7 The sculpture has been stolen.
8 The students have passed.

105
2 Nearly £50,000 was taken from the hotel safe.
3 Several of the bedrooms were also broken into.
4 Articles of value were removed.
5 Several pieces of equipment were damaged.
6 The chef was injured.
7 He was left lying unconscious on the floor.
8 The thieves were arrested early this morning.

106
2 won't be overheard
3 wouldn't have been sacked
4 is never answered … are kept … have been written
5 had been watered … had been cut
6 is suspected … has been arrested … is being questioned … will be identified
7 was being reorganised … had been moved

107
2 it **belonged** to my grandmother
3 *OK*
4 It**'s being repaired** this week.
5 The bridge **collapsed**
6 someone **will get burnt/ burned**
7 it **didn't refer** to you
8 *OK*
9 your bag **had disappeared**
10 **are not allowed** in the jacuzzi

English Grammar in Use Supplementary Exercises

Key

108
2 We've been shown
3 we've seen
4 We were driven
5 could be seen
6 have risen
7 was founded
8 I'd been warned
9 We were given
10 which are kept
11 was sent
12 hated
13 behaved
14 get sacked
15 we'll be joining
16 They were discovered
17 to be shown
18 get connected

109
2 was kept waiting for half an hour by my hairdresser
3 must be paid by the students
4 could have been written by your brother
5 is supplied by solar panels
6 were employed every week
7 weren't informed that there had been a mistake
8 be sent by your company next year
9 was worried by the news about the war
10 hasn't been claimed by anybody
11 ever been asked for your opinion
12 shouldn't be allowed to watch that kind of TV programme
13 must be worn by all visitors
14 must have been changed
15 will the food for the party be delivered

110
2 's been closed / has been closed
3 's being held / is being held there
4 it's being organised / it is being organised / it's organised / it is organised
5 they'd been seen / they had been seen / they were seen
6 they were flown
7 's going to be / is going to be / will be surrounded
8 we won't be invited
9 will probably be cancelled
10 were being recruited / were recruited
11 we'll be employed / we will be employed
12 to be allowed

111
2 'll/will get
3 is
4 got
5 got
6 are
7 gets
8 got
9 are
10 got

112
2 is thought to be short of money
3 was alleged to have cheated
4 is reported to be resigning
5 is expected to be finished soon
6 is generally considered (to be) too young to get married
7 was thought to have been destroyed
8 are believed to have been hiding for two weeks

113
2 was planned
3 was unloaded
4 was cooked
5 to be made
6 had been washed or were washed
7 was cleaned
8 was put
9 was being vacuumed
10 have been laid
11 have been arranged
12 have been mixed
13 will be opened
14 will be served

114
2 I'll have it cleaned.
3 I'll have them painted.
4 I'll have it rearranged.
5 I'll have it mended.
6 I'll have them emptied.
7 I'll have them washed.

115
2 I'm going to have a new operating system installed
3 are going to have her portrait painted
4 he's had a fine new house designed (by an architect)
5 I'm having blinds fitted on the windows
6 she had him followed (by a detective)
7 to have it straightened

116
3 When were you here before?
4 Why did you come then?
5 Why have you come this time?
6 Are you doing a tour now?
7 How many cities are you going to visit? or ... will you visit?
8 What do you want to do after that?
9 Do you have a message for your fans?

117
2 how much this guidebook is / costs
3 where the postcards are
4 what time/when the sports centre closes
5 how this timetable works / how to use this timetable
6 where I can get/find free Internet access
7 when the music festival is / when the music festival takes place
8 how old the castle is / when the castle was built

118
2 Is one with a sea view available?
3 have you heard about the special offer we are running at the moment?
4 Why don't you take advantage of it?
5 What have I got to do to qualify for it?
6 How much will it be for bed and breakfast?

Key

7 Shall I give you my credit card number now?
8 Would you like me to email confirmation of your reservation to you?

119
2 how much do you weigh? / what do you weigh?
3 how tall are you?
4 What do you do (for a living)? / What's your job/occupation?
5 do you take regular exercise? / do you exercise regularly?
6 Do you do any sport?
7 Do you smoke?
8 Have you (ever) tried to give (it) up?

120
2 What **does** this word mean?
3 How much **does it cost** to fly to Australia from here?
4 We can't remember where **we left** our car.
5 OK
6 Would you like to explain what **your problem is**?
7 How long did it **take you** to get here?
8 Now I know why **you didn't** tell me what you were buying!
9 OK
10 Why **don't young people** show more respect to the elderly?

121
I **want** to move out. **My** sister **has found** a flat **we can/could** share, and **we looked** round it **last week**. It **has just been decorated** and **we liked** it very much, but **we've been asked / we were asked** to pay a month's rent in advance. Unfortunately, because **I'm working** part-time and **I don't earn** much money, **I haven't saved** enough for the deposit. **I'm going to get** a new job. **I'm being interviewed tomorrow**, so **I have / I've got** to buy some new clothes for the interview.

122
2 'd been / had been
3 'd had / had had
4 'd worked / had worked
5 'd needed / had needed
6 'd wanted / had wanted
7 'd visited / had visited
8 'd been / had been
9 'd spent / had spent
10 'd been / had been
11 'd brought / had brought
12 'd become / had become
13 thought
14 had been
15 was

123
2 wasn't
3 'd come / had come
4 was doing
5 was going to visit *or* would visit
6 wanted
7 had
8 to come

124
2 was upset
3 wasn't interested
4 had promised *or* promised
5 hadn't turned up or didn't turn up
6 didn't want to see you
7 had had or had
8 didn't believe
9 had tried or tried
10 had come
11 had tried or tried
12 if she believed
13 would talk
14 was going to be

125
Example answers:
would dance to live bands every night.
(that) room service was available and they served an international menu in the dining-room.
(that) we'd love the private beach.
(that) a fitness centre had been added to the hotel's facilities, the tennis courts could be booked free of charge and guests could use the nearby golf course free of charge.

126
2 Where do you come from?
3 I come from Dublin.
4 That's where I was born too.
5 I've been a fan of yours for ages.
6 That's very good to hear.
7 Are you going to the concert tonight?
8 We want to, but we haven't been able to get tickets.
9 Are the tickets sold out?
10 They've sold all but the most expensive ones and we can't afford those.
11 Can they have some at the cheaper price?

127
The email should use reported speech and reported question structures in the same way as the underlined words in Exercise 126.

128
2 (me) where I was going to spend the holiday
3 (me) what I would do when I left school
4 how the security guard knew his/her name
5 (me) if/whether I had an appointment
6 whether/if his wife had seen the blue memory stick
7 why she hadn't phoned him
8 Rosemary whether/if she would carry his laptop for him
9 the receptionist when he could see the doctor

129
2 did you say
3 tell
4 to tell
5 would you say
6 to say
7 told
8 told
9 wouldn't say
10 won't say
11 've already told / have already told
12 tell me *or* say
13 tell

English Grammar in Use Supplementary Exercises

Key

130
2 told
3 said
4 told
5 had said
6 to tell
7 said
8 Tell
9 was saying *or* said

131
2 OK
3 She **was telling us about** her fascinating trip *or* She **was talking about** her fascinating trip
4 OK
5 the receptionist **told us that** the hotel *or* **said that** the hotel
6 visitors **not to touch** the exhibits
7 OK

132
3 entering
4 living
5 to bring
6 to be living
7 working
8 to support

133
2 to ride
3 setting off
4 to lose
5 hitting
6 to try
7 having lost *or* losing
8 to raise
9 to find

134
Example answers:
2 to see *or* to visit
3 postponing *or* putting off *or* delaying
4 writing *or* doing
5 going *or* changing *or* switching
6 to deliver
7 to send *or* to post
8 to do *or* to post
9 losing *or* offending
10 emailing
11 to help
12 to join
13 replying

135
2 Hugo to do fifty press-ups.
3 the cashier to hand over the money
4 buying Della the drums / buying the drums (for Della)
5 Charlie finish his homework
6 to reach the shampoo
7 washing *or* to be washed
8 Sandy (to) lay the table

136
2 being shouted
3 to sack
4 to have worked
5 changing
6 to say
7 being
8 to get
9 to pass
10 help
11 to discuss
12 asking
13 to have known

137
Example answers:
2 I learnt to swim at the age of six.
3 I can't help getting angry when I see someone being treated unfairly.
4 I don't mind washing up, but I hate vacuuming the floors.
5 I sometimes pretend to be listening to what the boss is saying when really I'm just daydreaming.
6 I always encourage people to read books which I have enjoyed reading myself.
7 I remember going to the circus when I was a small child.
8 I enjoy swimming even though I'm not very good at it.
9 I expect to have passed my driving test by the end of next year.
10 I've given up going to discos because they're too noisy.

138
2 a   3 f   4 c   5 g
6 e   7 d

139
2 by checking the instructions
3 spending too long on one question
4 trying to see how your friends are getting on
5 by allowing time to check all your answers
6 cheating in the long run

140
Example answers:
2 buying fast food every day
3 sitting at home watching TV
4 offering to help you
5 helping people who don't want it
6 telling someone where you're going
7 being late
8 ordering goods online

141
3 go
4 waking
5 arrive
6 finding
7 spending
8 say
9 being

142
3 of looking
4 to risk
5 in persuading
6 to hearing
7 to have
8 to achieve
9 for letting *or* to have let
10 of sending
11 in going
12 about forgetting *or* for forgetting
13 to forget
14 from sending
15 to remember
16 to forget

143
4 had been murdered
5 didn't love
6 didn't murder
7 wanted
8 had *or* was having
9 asked
10 was watching
11 told
12 called
13 noticed

Key

14 had expected *or* had been expecting
15 answered
16 was shouting
17 were obviously having
18 took
19 shouting
20 had gone
21 to go
22 didn't want
23 heard
24 came
25 was still talking
26 heard
27 wasn't shouting
28 phoned
29 talked
30 told
31 had decided
32 was watching
33 take
34 spilt/spilled
35 was pouring
36 didn't want
37 crept
38 decided
39 never tell
40 see/'m going to see
41 had had
42 usually takes
43 took
44 went
45 saw
46 was walking
47 saw
48 was standing
49 didn't see *or* couldn't see
50 was talking
51 hadn't answered
52 reached
53 remembered
54 was playing *or* was going to play
55 walked
56 met
57 reached
58 was looking
59 called
60 was
61 had planned
62 had been visiting
63 let
64 seemed
65 showed
66 shouting
67 were having *or* had been having
68 stopped
69 went
70 had already left
71 got
72 to explain
73 to have
74 didn't listen *or* wouldn't listen
75 was
76 didn't know
77 was talking
78 realised
79 arguing
80 left
81 seeing
82 weren't
83 is
84 have lived *or* have been living
85 used to have *or* had
86 bought
87 earning *or* to earn
88 went
89 ran
90 lost
91 was looking
92 met
93 was walking
94 seemed
95 was looking
96 hadn't seen
97 went
98 found
99 wasn't
100 didn't even go
101 had found out
102 means
103 left *or* must have left
104 was going to leave *or* was leaving
105 to murder
106 can't have walked *or* couldn't have walked
107 met
108 was still being shouted at
109 has been telling *or* is telling
110 made

144
3 a biscuit 5 an omelette
4 OK   6 OK

145
2 an egg   6 a roll / bread
3 a sandwich   7 pasta
4 a banana   8 sauce
5 soup   9 an orange

146
The diary entry should be similar to Jane's. Check carefully your use of a/an before the names of food and drinks.

147
3 the **traffic is** awful
4 because of **bad behaviour**
5 OK
6 Rebecca had her **hair** cut so short
7 the **furniture is** very old-fashioned
8 I give you **some advice** / **a piece of advice**
9 OK
10 wasn't **a pleasant experience**

148
3 room
4 experience
5 scenery
6 weather
7 day
8 rooms
9 paper
10 experiences
11 views
12 paper *or* papers

149
2 the   9 the   16 a
3 the   10 The   17 the
4 a   11 the   18 the
5 an   12 the   19 some
6 The   13 a   20 an
7 the   14 a
8 a   15 some

Example answers:
21 There is a parking space next to the road and a small lawn with some trees round it.
22 A path goes round the building from the road, past the kitchen window to the patio.

English Grammar in Use Supplementary Exercises

Key

150
Check carefully your use of a/an/the/some.

151
2 the	6 the	10 a
3 the	7 a	11 a
4 a	8 The	12 the
5 a	9 the	

152
4 The	10 the	16 the
5 the	11 –	17 –
6 –	12 –	18 the
7 –	13 the	19 the
8 the	14 –	20 the
9 the	15 –	

153
Check carefully your use of the.

154
… and ~~the~~ Malaysia and then go on to the Philippines, for a conference about ~~the~~ global warming.
ROYAL VISIT ~~The~~ King Juan Carlos of ~~the~~ Spain arrives today for a short visit to the United Kingdom. After lunch with the Queen at ~~the~~ Windsor Castle, he will open an exhibition at the National Gallery in ~~the~~ Trafalgar Square and in the evening he will have talks with ~~the~~ businessmen.
RAIL CRASH … The injured have been taken to ~~the~~ Southampton Hospital. For ~~the~~ information phone the police on 01273 01023.

155
Example answers:
5 All of them were wearing sandals.
6 None of them was wearing socks.
7 Both (of) the men had beards. *or* Both men …
8 Both of them had short hair.
9 Both of them were wearing belts.
10 Neither of the men was wearing a hat.
11 Neither of them was wearing a jacket.
12 One of the men had a newspaper.

156
Example answers:
5 None of my friends lives in the country.
6 Lots of our neighbours have pets.
7 All politicians are ambitious.
8 Some of my cousins are very silly.
9 Neither of my parents enjoys noisy parties.

157
2 none of
3 any of
4 half (of) … all of … any of
5 most … a few
6 much
7 each
8 None of
9 Few
10 all (of) … each … none of

158
2 I **have none** / I h**aven't got any**
3 if **anybody gets** left
4 There **are no** good clubs, nothing! *or* There **aren't any** good clubs, nothing!
5 because he **had few** friends
6 because **all the information** you gave me
7 I could have **any seat**
8 she has **so much** homework
9 embarrassed that **everyone** / **everybody knows** my problem
10 I'd spend **half of it**

159
2 anything
3 All
4 both
5 none of the
6 them
7 every weekend
8 Neither of
9 somebody
10 somewhere
11 little
12 a few
13 no
14 anywhere
15 the whole
16 no

160
2 Antonio Stradivari was an Italian who made wonderful violins.
3 Ibn Battuta was a Moroccan who travelled through Africa and Asia.
4 Marie Tussaud was a Swiss woman who opened a waxworks museum.
5 Valentina Tereshkova is a Russian who was the first female astronaut.
6 Katsushika Hokusai was a Japanese man who made the famous print *The Great Wave off Kanagawa*.
7 Joseph Niépce was a Frenchman who produced the first permanent photograph.

161
3 whose	8 –
4 who/that	9 –
5 –	10 that
6 –	11 –
7 where	12 where

162
Example answers:
3 where the music is no good for dancing
4 who play football *or* volleyball
5 which aren't in fashion
6 in which there is plenty of action
7 whose parents don't give them any money
8 to whom I can say anything
9 which takes good photos
10 which involved travelling

163
3 a 4 a 5 b 6 a 7 b
8 a 9 b 10 a

164
2 good
3 efficiently
4 hard
5 surprisingly

Key

6 quickly
7 lately
8 fluent
9 near
10 pleasant
11 busy
12 easily
13 different
14 absolutely
15 good
16 accurate

165
3 seemed **unnecessarily complicated**
4 if you tried **hard**
5 OK
6 she speaks **perfect French** *or* she speaks **French perfectly**
7 an **exceptionally** demanding job
8 she's **well** enough
9 OK
10 a very **well**-paid job

166
2 the lowest
3 better than
4 worse than *or* not as well as / not so well as
5 higher ... than
6 less
7 the same ... as
8 more than
9 less than

167
Example answers:
4 Jill collected more than Alex *or* Wayne.
5 Bronwen collected the same amount as Jill.
6 Wayne collected the least paper.
7 Alex didn't collect as much as Bronwen, but he collected more than Wayne.
8 Jill collected less than Flora, but more than Alex.

168
4 no faster than
5 the cheapest
6 the most expensive
7 furthest

8 much easier than
9 the best
10 not as warm as / not so warm as
11 later
12 earlier here than
13 (any) faster
14 as fast as
15 older than mine
16 (any) better
17 worse
18 as much money as / so much money as

169
2 We went to the cinema and we also had a meal.
3 My sister plays volleyball in the park in summer.
4 She's worked for that company since she left school.
5 If you order the trainers online now, they'll be delivered by post tomorrow.
6 He sends his girlfriend an email from his office every lunchtime.
7 When the flowers were delivered, was there a note with them?
8 We were all late for work because of the traffic jam.
9 I'm definitely going to Zurich soon.
10 The meal was lovely. My friends had even asked the restaurant to make a birthday cake for me.

170
3 Craig has occasionally worked from home.
4 Angela isn't usually in the office at lunchtime.
5 John doesn't usually eat with his colleagues.
6 Craig usually drinks a lot of coffee.
7 Angela has hardly ever been off sick.
8 John hardly ever answers emails promptly.
9 Craig is hardly ever in a bad temper.

171
3 Well, the downstairs ones are always locked.
4 We even have a lock on the little one in the hall.
5 most of the windows were probably locked
6 They were all locked on Friday.
7 I knew we would both be out all day
8 I certainly didn't

172
3 doesn't even belong to one
4 has never been there
5 often has a few days off at this time of year
6 has almost finished it

173
3 For   8 in
4 until   9 for
5 By/At   10 at
6 During/In 11 during
7 by

174
Example answers:
1 in May *or* on 8th May
2 in 2001
3 at about nine o'clock in the evening
4 in summer
5 after dinner
6 on my birthday
7 for five years

175
3 At   8 while   13 at
4 –   9 for   14 –
5 until 10 on   15 at/for
6 in   11 until   16 during
7 at/by 12 by   17 by

176
2 at   5 on   8 on
3 in   6 at   9 at
4 in   7 to

177
2 on   7 in
3 in   8 in
4 at   9 on
5 on
6 at

English Grammar in Use Supplementary Exercises 135

Key

178
2 of
3 to
4 to
5 for
6 with
7 in
8 for
9 on
10 on
11 as
12 with

179
2 in the shade
3 on a special diet
4 by credit card
5 by recent college graduates
6 at 20 km per hour
7 in capital letters
8 by a wasp
9 like the last one
10 as a motorcycle messenger

180
Example answers:
2 for rich people
3 of representing their country
4 in sport
5 about going to the dentist
6 on how much sleep I get
7 at my little brother
8 in fairies

181
2 for giving up
3 on their advice
4 of making
5 of her behaviour
6 with her
7 with herself
8 in changing her opinion
9 of Helen
10 on doing
11 of behaving

182
Example answers:
2 e The bus crashed into the railings.
3 a The square was full of market stalls.
4 f The minibus belonged to a group of tourists.
5 c They borrowed the car from a local family.
6 d They blamed the accident on a pedestrian.
7 h The owner was upset about having to sell his car.
8 g The driver apologised for taking the wrong road.

183
Example answers:
2 's going to knock them over / is going to knock them over
3 's going to wake him/her up / is going to wake him/her up
4 's going to blow them out / is going to blow them out
5 's going to hand them out / is going hand them out
6 's going to clean (it) up / is going to clean (it) up
7 's going to turn it off / is going to turn it off
8 's going to take them off / is going to take them off

184
2 from
3 with
4 with
5 on
6 to
7 to
8 with
9 to
10 with

185
2 get away
3 get back
4 getting in
5 get on *or* are getting on
6 get on
7 get by

186
2 taken away
3 were taken in
4 take down
5 took up
6 take up
7 took off *or* had taken off

187
2 's going on / is going on
3 go on
4 'll go back / will go back
5 's away / is away *or* 's gone away / has gone away
6 's has gone out / has gone out
7 'm going (to go) out / am going (to go) out

188
2 put on
3 be put back
4 put on
5 put off
6 put down
7 put on

189
2 turned out
3 turned up
4 turned out
5 turn up
6 turned off
7 turn down

190
2 fill it in
3 do not tear it up
4 hand it back
5 leave any information out / leave out any information
6 cross it out
7 rub it out
8 being held up

191
2 found out *or* has found out
3 has broken down
4 put up with
5 shows off *or* has showed off
6 lets me down *or* has let me down
7 bring their daughter Mimi up / bring up their daughter Mimi
8 won't keep her away
9 have fallen out with
10 run away from

192
2 pay them back
3 close down
4 ripped them off
5 had been held up *or* were held up
6 do them up
7 brought the subject up / brought up the subject

193
2 went on
3 went off
4 blew up
5 drive away
6 gave up
7 dropped off
8 riding off

194
2 worked out
3 plugged in
4 left out
5 carry on
6 turned it down
7 put up with
8 found out
9 put off
10 cutting down

195
She used to ~~invent~~ **come up with** all kinds of excuses when she was younger. Now, she's ~~left~~ **dropped out of** college

~~without finishing her course~~. Her father says he won't ~~tolerate~~ **put up with** her behaviour any longer, but I bet Ruth ~~won't be punished for~~ **will get away with** it, as usual. If I ~~disappointed~~ **let down** my parents like she does, I'd be in real trouble!

196
2 put
3 was held
4 crossed
5 were brought
6 (had) let
7 making
8 set

197
Example answers:
2 keep up with her
3 run out of
4 made it up
5 get on with it *or* hurry up
6 put it up *or* try it out
7 let us down
8 got on with them *or* gets on with them

198
Example answers:
2 off for the playground carrying their skateboards
3 off revising for as long as possible
4 on several coats, but none of them was the right size
5 off two hours late
6 off her phone when the film began
7 on talking all through the film
8 off in front of the visitors

199
Example answers:
2 down the chance of a job in Hong Kong
3 up with the noise for as long as possible
4 up oil painting when he retired
5 down the wall because it was dangerous
6 up the gambler who hadn't paid his debts
7 up to buy a flat
8 down when the new supermarket was opened

200
Example answers:
2 The prisoner climbed out of the broken window.
3 The new student joined in with the rest of the class.
4 Air travellers must check in at least one hour before their flight.
5 The picture has been cut out of a fashion magazine.
6 The schoolboy let himself in with his key and made himself a sandwich.
7 My secretary will sort out the documents you need for the meeting.
8 The investigation was carried out by a senior police officer.